What others

The Hoodlum Preacher...

"The Hoodlum Preacher helped get me through some discouraging times while being imprisoned. The book confirmed the fact that I can accomplish anything, as long as I have faith."

-Project Pat, Hip-Hop Artist

"I always knew God's power to heal and transform. Burton Barr Jr. is living proof."

-Maya Azucena, National Recording Artist

"How can a man be born again? Read this book to find out how a man caught in the grip of his own flesh and blood was born again through water and the spirit. Riveting and inspiring, this book offers a brave model from which all sinners, great and small and most of us in the middle, can gain confidence in themselves as they deepen their faith in God. Some books make faith sound like an abstract notion; this book makes it as lively and urgent as the thunderstorm of God's grace that breaks over all of us every day".

-Dr. Eugene C. Kennedy, Author

"It is amazing what can be accomplished with a little love and a lot of faith. Never say you can't! It is the painful details that prove we can. Rev. Barr's courageous journey should serve as inspiration for one and all."

-Sharia Kharif, Author of Tomorrow's Sun and Tears in the Wind

To Bro. Boogie
You are blessed

[signature]

THE HOODLUM PREACHER

by Burton Barr, Jr.

Kobalt Books
St. Louis, MO / Philadelphia, PA

Library of Congress Control Number: 2006921151

For information:
Kobalt Books
P.O. Box 1062,
Bala Cynwyd, PA 19004
Printed in the U.S.A
www.kobaltbooks.com

Cover Design by Stephen Bruce
Book Description by Sharia Kharif
Book edited by Kesha Mixon, Sharia Kharif and Eve Lane
Scripture quotations are from:
The Holy Bible, NIV ©1984, Thomas Nelson, Inc.
Song lyric quotations:
"*I Want To Know What Love Is*", by Mick Jones-Foreigner
©1984 Somerset Songs Publishing, Inc. (ASCAP)

Published by Kobalt Books L.L.C.
An original publication of Kobalt Books L.L.C.

This book is dedicated to the memory
of my loving parents,
Rev. Burton Barr Sr. and Mary Jane Barr

To my beautiful and adorable wife,
Charlotte Anne Barr,
who I love so much

To my lovely daughter,
Andrea,
who has always loved me

To my son,
Marcus,
a remarkable young man

To my three precious
Granddaughters,
Asia
Amia
&
Arnisia

And
To my five wonderful new daughters
Marlene
Anita
Chiriga
Chene
&
Jeseca

To all of my many new grandchildren
And
To the West Side Missionary Baptist Church Family
I love you all

TABLE OF CONTENTS

ACKNOWLEDGEMENTS

There are so many people that I want to thank for encouraging me to share my life and experiences in the form of a book. First of all, thanks to my church family, the West Side Missionary Baptist Church. They told me that everyone needed to hear my story.

Thanks to my pastor and friend, Rev. Dr. Ronald L. Bobo, Sr. for his support. He constantly encouraged me to write this book. I think he told my story more than I did.

Thanks to my cousin, Quincy Simms, who was always calling and asking me, "Are you finished writing your book yet?"

Thanks to Denita Robinson, who finally convinced me to sit down, start writing, and helped me find a publisher.

Thanks to Cedric Mixon, for taking a chance on me and agreeing to publish this book.

Thanks to Sandi Sims, a true friend. She has been there for me in the good times and the bad.

Most of all, I thank God for His grace and mercy.

FOREWORD

God has deemed it necessary to make each vessel in His kingdom a unique and privileged entity. I can see His creative wonder in the person and work of Burton Barr Jr. His is a story that will not be soon forgotten because God has made him in such a powerful and irreproducible fashion that others may imitate, but they will never duplicate the peculiar mixture of gifts, empowerment and diligence that make up this courageous Man of God. I say that he is courageous because of the extraordinary obstacles that he has had to overcome in order to trust God for victory in his life. His struggles have taken him to the lowest of lows. But those same struggles have been the catalyst and the catapult to hurl him over his challenges unto victory in Jesus Christ. As the reader digests the humor and sadness, reverence and awe that is skillfully and dynamically ensconced within these pages one might tend to forget that this is not a novel or a writing of fiction that is before us. It is a real life story, with real situations and with an authentic and practical message for people of every walk of life. Your life will be profoundly impacted by his. It has been both my privilege and my pleasure to serve as his pastor, prayer partner and friend.

Having known Burton Barr for the past decade, I have also come to know the power of God in transforming a life. For those who have determined that God cannot use them due to the failures of the past, this is a book that will give you renewed hope and encouragement. You can get up again, and again, and again. How often we have seen people who have fallen into sin and as a result, into hopelessness and despair. This could have been the plight of this man of God as well, but God's grace and mercy have no boundaries. We now see a man who is able to once again preach with power and conviction and minister to the prisoner, to the brokenhearted and to the hopeless with a compassion that could only come from a man whose heart is in the hand of God. From a preacher, to a hoodlum and back again. To God be the Glory!

Rev. Ronald L. Bobo Sr., D. Min.
West Side Missionary Baptist Church / St. Louis, Missouri

INTRODUCTION

It was a cool, crisp Chicago evening in September of 1985. I was feeling kind of good about myself because I had just pulled off, what I thought was, one of the sweetest con games I had played in a long time. It would keep me out of jail and put some money in my pocket at the same time. That was what I did for a living. I played games on people that separated them from their money or their merchandise. But I wasn't a big time con man like the guys in the movie "The Sting" or the men Iceberg Slim talked about in his book, "Trick Baby." I wasn't trying to be either. At that stage of my life, I was just trying to get enough money to feed my $200.00 a day drug habit. When I say $200.00, that's just an average. There were many days that I spent well over $500.00, and there were some days that I couldn't even raise a hundred.

I was sitting in my living room that evening watching Smokey Robinson's new TV program with my brother, Ralph. We called him "Weasel," because he was short and fast. We all had nicknames in my neighborhood. Mine was "Bub", short for Bubba. My childhood friend, Richie, gave it to me. His favorite baseball player was Bubba Philips, the former third baseman for the Chicago Cubs. Richie's family was one of the last white families to move out of the neighborhood.

Ralph and I have always been close. We've had our differences over the years, but what brothers don't? We used to love to get together and watch sports on TV or listen to some jazz while we were getting high. Ralph didn't shoot up like I did. As a matter of fact, he hated for me to do it. But that was my thing, "Speed balling." Speed balling is mixing heroin and cocaine together and either shooting or snorting it.

Ralph's thing was smoking crack. They called it freebasing back then because they would take some cocaine, mix it with baking soda and water, and then cook it in a test tube. Most people had never heard of freebasing until Richard Pryor almost burned himself up while he was doing it. After that, everybody wanted to try it. But that just goes to show you the mentality of the average drug user. If someone died of an overdose because they had some drugs that were too strong, everybody wanted some of that, because they knew it had to be some good stuff.

To me, freebasing was just wasting good cocaine. So whenever Ralph and I got together, we would just drink whisky and beer, and smoke reefer. That's what we were doing when the doorbell rang. Ralph started towards the door, but I thought it might have been Shelia, my lady friend at the time, so I decided to answer it myself. The building we lived in was the two family flat where we had grown up. My father lived on the first floor, and Ralph and I lived upstairs.

When I got to the door, I pulled back the shade and saw two policemen standing on the porch. One of them was in uniform; the other one was a detective. I figured they were there to arrest me, but I wasn't worried. I was sure I could talk them out of it; I had done it many times before. When I turned the lock and pushed the door open, I put on my best smile.

I didn't even get the door completely open before one of my hands was cuffed and I was being pulled out onto the front porch. They finished handcuffing me and informed me that they had a warrant for my arrest. As I was being taken away, I noticed they had come in different cars. The uniformed officer was a Chicago city policeman. The detective was from one of the suburbs and had to be accompanied by a city officer in order to serve a warrant inside of the city limits. I was put in the car and taken to Oak Park, Illinois.

While I was being booked, I found out that the sweet con game I had played earlier that day had backfired. I didn't know that the manager of the store where I had passed some bad checks at earlier in the week had found out how I operated. So while I was planning phase two of my con, he was at the police station filing charges against me. I also found out that I had another warrant from another suburb, so my bond was $11,000. I needed $1,100 to get out of jail. I didn't have it.

When I got to my cell, I thought I was in "Jail Heaven." I had never been in a hold-over cell like that in my life, and I had been in a lot of them. Most of them were crowded, noisy, open cells with cold steel benches. Most of the time the benches were so crowded, prisoners had to sleep on the floor. And you had to wait forever for someone to let you out to use the phone.

This was more like a single room. It was nice and warm, and there was a bed in there with a mattress, a pillow, and a blanket. There was a telephone in there too. When I looked around, I realized I had been hanging out in the wrong jails. I decided right then, that from that point on, I was going to commit all of my crimes in the suburbs, preferably Oak Park. Prisoners had it going on out there.

I talked on the phone most of the night. But I wasn't calling people, trying to get bond money; I was calling to tell them about that fancy jail cell I was in. One of the people I called was Sandi, an ex girlfriend of mine who lived in St. Louis. Although we were no longer together, we still remained friends, kind of. You've got to remember, I still had the mind of a hustler and a con. Sandi was a beautiful, loving woman. But she came into my life at the wrong time. I had been hurt by so many women, my heart had become calloused. I had decided that I was going to be the one doing the hurting. Unfortunately, Sandi was one of my victims. She really didn't deserve that.

We tend to do that to each other sometimes. We are so focused on our own hurt feelings that we don't see the pain that we are causing someone else. It's kind of like an automobile accident. Even if the accident is our fault, the first thing we do is look at the damage that was done to our car. We are not that concerned about the other person's car. It is the same when we sin against God. The first thing we do is look at how it has damaged our lives. We are not really concerned with how we hurt the God who loves us.

When I woke up the next morning, I couldn't believe the breakfast they gave me. It was an Egg McMuffin with a hash brown and orange juice from the McDonald's next door. All we ever got for breakfast in the city jails was a stale, dried-up Honey Bun.

I went to court later that morning and was bound over for trial. Since I was not able to make bond, I was sent to the Cook County Jail. That is where people are held until they either bond out or go to court. If you are convicted in court and sentenced to

11

do time, you might do it there if your sentence is one year or less. Anything over a year, including one day, you go to the penitentiary.

The county jail is located on the corner of 26th and California Street. Ironically, it is only two blocks from my old high school, Carter H. Harrison, which was located on 24th and California Street.

After a brief stay in Division 5, I was moved to Division 2. That was the minimum-security section of the jail. It is a two-story building with two open dorms on each floor. There were about 40 or 50 inmates in each dorm. The older, more mature prisoners were housed on the first floor. The second floor was known as "Gladiator School." It was reserved for the "Thunder Cats." Those were the young gang bangers who spent most of their time fighting. We could hear them throwing beds, tables, chairs, benches, and everything else that wasn't nailed down. Sometimes it sounded like they were coming through the floor. If anyone on the first floor got out of hand or gave one of the C.O.s (Correctional Officers) any trouble, they were transferred upstairs to Gladiator School.

I learned something while I was in Cook County. The C.O.s didn't really run the jail. The gangs did. The C.O.s controlled the overall system as far as telling the inmates what to do and when to do it, therefore, maintaining some sense of order. But when it came to the individual dorms or wings or cellblocks, they were definitely run by the gangs. I learned that the minute I stepped into "D" dorm.

There were three of us that were taken to "D" dorm. The first person I saw when we walked in was Cochise. He was tall, thin, and crazy looking. He was not wearing a shirt and his pants were hanging well below his waist with his boxers showing, although "sagging" was not yet in style back then. He had another inmate pinned against the wall and was all up in his face. Then he threw him across the room onto the floor and shouted, "If you ever do that again, I'll tear your head off." Then he looked over at us and said, "What ya'll looking at?" We just turned and went our separate ways, looking for the bunks we were assigned.

I later found out that Cochise was the "shot caller" for "Folks" in "D" dorm. "Folks" is a group of Chicago area gangs

12

that are united. The inmate that Cochise was beating up was a member of "Peoples," another group of gangs, and the arch enemies of "Folks." In "D" dorm, "Folks" out numbered "Peoples" 10 to 1.

During that time, in the Chicago jail and prison system, there were three categories of inmates, Peoples, Folks, and Neutrons. Neutron is another word for neutral, meaning they were not in either gang. Neutrons were the minority. Ain't that something? Being black, I had been a minority all of my life. Now, there I was in the Cook County Jail where almost everyone was black, and I was still a minority. That wasn't the first time I had been locked down, so I was able to adjust.

The brother in the bunk next to mine slept all of the time. He would get up when it was time to go to the mess hall to eat, but when he got back to the dorm, he just went right back to sleep. I knew how it was; street life can take its toll on you. Sometimes the police are really doing some people a favor when they lock them up. That's the only time they get any rest. So in a sense, they didn't arrest us, they rescued us.

Prison is a culture of hardness. You can never show any sign of weakness or fear. If you do, the predators will sense it, and they will be on you like a pack of dogs. If you are challenged in any way, you must meet it head on. Smart inmates try to avoid certain situations and certain people. Their goal is to do their time and stay away from trouble. But if trouble comes to them, they deal with it.

On my second day in "D" dorm, I was lying across my bunk. Since it was an open dorm, I made it a habit to always lie on my back. I didn't want anyone looking at my booty and getting any crazy ideas. We had just returned from lunch and I didn't want to watch TV. As I stated earlier, the gangs controlled the jail, and that included the TV set. They liked to watch the soaps after "Oprah" and the other morning programs went off.

I was just lying there with my blanket over my face trying to keep the light out of my eyes. I didn't want to see anyone and I didn't want anyone to see me. I was angry and feeling sorry for myself. My birthday was coming up soon and it was beginning to look like I would be spending another one of them in jail. I was really getting tired of that.

13

THE HOODLUM PREACHER

I heard Cochise's voice. He was talking to one of his soldiers. I heard their footsteps and their voices coming closer and closer. I started praying, "Please Lord, let them keep going." But they stopped right by my bunk. I had spent two days trying to avoid this crazy man, and now he was standing over me, with Larry, his right hand man. All of a sudden it got real hot under that blanket. I was sweating and praying and making all kinds of deals with God.

While they were standing there, I heard Larry say, "Who is that?" Cochise said, "That's just some old preacher that's running from God." Then I heard them walking away. That messed me up. I had been a preacher, but I had quit years ago. I didn't know how Cochise knew. God had called me to preach, but I didn't want to do it anymore. So Cochise was right when he said I was running from God. I was a fugitive, but I wasn't the only one. Our jails and prisons are full of fugitives. Some of them are fugitives, running from justice. Some of them are fugitives running from God.

My friend, Richie, had a little brother named Michael. When we were younger, Michael used to aggravate some of us older boys and then run into his house before we could catch him. Once, Michael did something that made me angry, but that day I caught him before he was able to get home, and I beat the mess out of him.

Afterwards, it dawned on me that I had one little brother, but Michael had four big brothers, so I ran home. That evening, while we were eating dinner, the doorbell rang. Thinking it was Michael's brothers, I jumped up and ran out the back door. My father caught up with me and asked what was going on. After I told him what had happened, he said, "Son, when you are in trouble, you are supposed to run to your house, not away from your house."

That is how Satan tricks us. When we mess up or get into trouble, we leave the church because of embarrassment or we don't know if we will be forgiven. But that is the time that we should run to God and to the church, instead of running from them.

Later that night, we were all sitting around watching TV when Cochise called me off to the side. He said, "What are you doing in here Preacher? You don't belong here." I started telling him about my crimes and some of the things I had done, trying to impress him and show him how bad I was, but he just started laughing. He said, "You know you ain't suppose to be doing that stuff."

I went back to my seat and started watching TV again. Just then, one of the C.O.s came in and handed Cochise bags of food. Some of the C.O.s were gang members that had never been arrested. All of the gang members started making sandwiches and eating. It had been a long time since dinner, and I was hungry too. But I wasn't part of the gang. Cochise looked up from his sandwich and said, "Hey Preacher, are you hungry?" When I said that I was, he told someone to give me a sandwich. But what they gave me was a jailhouse donut and some bread. I'd had one of those donuts in the mess hall before; they were terrible. They were not sweet at all.

I was looking at the donut and bread wondering, "What am I supposed to do with this?" when Cochise asked me if I had ever had a donut sandwich before. I replied, "No." He told someone to show me how to make one. I thought they were playing a joke on me. Someone told me to put some butter and jelly on the bread, put the donut in between. I tried it. It was great.

We were given donuts at least twice a week with our breakfast. From then on I always made sandwiches with them. Whenever we had something for lunch or dinner that I didn't like, I would trade it with another inmate for their donut sandwich. My niece, Christine, teases me because to this day, I still eat them. Donut sandwiches.

After everyone had eaten that night, Cochise called me in front of everybody. He said, "Hey ya'll. This is 'Preacher'. He ain't Folks. He's a Neutron, but he's alright. I don't want nobody messing with him." So that became my name while I was in the Cook County Jail. Preacher. Cochise and I got to be pretty good friends. I asked him how he knew I had been a preacher? He said, "Anybody can look at you and tell you're a preacher." I didn't realize it at the time, but even in jail, God had His hand on me and was protecting me.

A few weeks later, detectives came to the jail and arrested me. Again. It was the dumbest thing I had ever heard of. How can

15

you arrest someone who is already in jail? It turned out that while I was in jail, stores in two other suburbs had pressed charges against me, so they added another $50,000 to my ransom, and moved me to Division 4, the more secure section of the jail. Things had gone from bad to worse. I figured God was angry with me, but I didn't think He was *this* angry.

Why was He so angry with me? After all, nobody's perfect. At least that's what I had always heard. The truth is, we do not live in a perfect world, and God did not create a perfect people. When God created man, He gave us the ability to choose how we live our lives. He gave us a tongue that can lie, a heart that can hate, hands that can kill, and thoughts that can lust. We were not born with a mouth that will not say things that hurt, or feet that will not follow the path of unrighteousness. We are however, blessed with a mind that can discern right from wrong.

The name Preacher followed me to Division 4. But something happened while I was in there that changed my life forever. Before I tell you about that, I want to go back a few years and tell you the story of how I became, "The Hoodlum Preacher."

CHAPTER ONE

The Call

I knew that I was going to be a preacher ever since I was nine years old. I was a junior usher at the Rose of Sharon Missionary Baptist Church located on 13th Street and Christiana Avenue, right down the street from our house. I loved to hear my first pastor, Reverend James A. Murphy, preach every Sunday morning. I would sit there with Ralph or my grandmother, listening to his every word. I even started my own church in my mother's kitchen one summer. Ralph was my only member. I would put on the robe that I was baptized in and preach to him everyday. He didn't have a choice since I was bigger than him. When I couldn't find him, I would go on the back porch and preach to our dog, Rex. I tried to baptize Rex in the bathtub one day. He didn't like that at all.

When I told my mother that I was going to be a preacher, she said I couldn't just decide that I was going to be a preacher. She said that God had to call me. So for the next day or two I stayed in the house, hanging around the phone waiting for God to call me. Needless to say, I never received that phone call, however, that didn't stop me from preaching to Ralph and Rex.

During my early teenage years, I strayed away from the church and started hanging out with some of the older boys in the neighborhood. I also discovered girls during that time. One girl in particular was Betty Jean, my very first love. She had big pretty eyes and the sweetest smile. She was very beautiful, and we had planned to get married some day.

She gave me a surprise party for my 16th birthday. It was the best party I'd ever had, but it wasn't much of a surprise. My friend, Fuzzy, was supposed to hang out with me until a certain time. Then he was supposed to take me to Elaine's apartment, where the party was being held. He ended up telling me what was going on before we got there. When we got to Elaine's, I acted surprised and we all had a good time.

My friends and I were not bad kids. We didn't steal or run around with gangs or anything. We just did typical teenage stuff. Some of us did dumb things, like getting drunk or ditching school. Whenever we ditched school, we stayed at my house because both of my parents worked. That's what we decided to do on the last school day before Christmas break in 1964.

There was Gip, Fuzzy, Joe, "who we called Gonzalez," and myself. Fuzzy had already dropped out of school. The rest of us were ditching. We had been drinking whiskey and playing records when we decided to go to the school and beat up some white boys. Now, our school, Harrison, was in a predominantly white neighborhood, and the majority of the students, about 80%, were white. Can you imagine four black, drunk, teenage boys riding a bus into an all white neighborhood to start a fight with some white boys in 1964? I told you, we did some dumb things. I don't think we even had any civil rights back then.

I stole my father's gun, a 32 revolver, to take with us. It was just for show, we only had one bullet. (Remember Barney Fife from the Andy Griffith show?) Gip held the gun. We got off the bus on 23rd and California and started a fight with some guys. We were quickly out numbered. When I realized how much trouble we were in, I started shouting, "Shoot 'em Gip. Shoot 'em." I was hoping they would hear me or see the gun and run, but they kept coming. When I looked around, there were about fifteen or twenty of them. I kept yelling, "Shoot um Gip. Shoot 'em."

But the gun had fallen through a hole that was in Gip's coat pocket and was trapped in the lining. When he finally got it out, Fuzzy grabbed it from him. Some of them saw the gun and started running. Fuzzy caught one of them and hit him in the head with it. When he did that, the gun went off. And all hell broke loose. I had never seen that many white people in my life. They were coming from everywhere, young and old. They were running out of their houses, and jumping out of cars. Some of them even came outside without shirts on. All of a sudden we heard gunshots. We knew it wasn't us; we didn't have any more bullets. So we started running. We saw a bus coming down California and jumped on it.

We ran to the back of the bus laughing and talking about what had just happened. We then realized that there were only three of us on the bus. Gip was missing. We started looking out the window trying to see him, but all we saw was a bunch of angry white people. We thought Gip was dead. They must have caught him and killed him.

When we got back to Christiana, we went to Gip's girlfriend Vivian's house to tell her about him. We drank more whiskey and beer. I got so drunk, I passed out. Somebody laid me across Vivian's bed. When I woke up, I didn't know where I was. The room was dark and extremely hot. I tried to stand up but fell against the wall, I slid sideways and got stuck between the radiator and the wall. The radiator was burning my stomach and chest, but every time I grabbed it to pull myself up, I burned my hands. I started yelling for help. Finally someone came and pulled me up. It was Gip. He had gotten away by running in the opposite direction. Remember that I was still drunk and thought Gip was dead. So when I saw him in that dark, hot room, you know where I thought we were, don't you? I was glad to find out that we were alive and not in hell.

Like I said, we were not bad kids, we were just misguided. Although there were a lot of churches in my neighborhood, most of their members were like guard dogs. In other words, they were territorial. The only time a guard dog will attack someone is if that person goes into his house, yard, or wanders into his territory. A guard dog will not go after a woman who is standing on the corner. He will not try to get to the gang-banger who is sitting on the porch across the street. He will not confront the kids in the neighborhood, or the wino who is standing in the alley. He will wait for them to come into his territory and then he will be all over them.

A lot of church members are the same way. They will not tell anyone outside of the sanctified walls of the church about the goodness of the Lord. They won't approach that woman who is standing on the corner. They won't reach out to that gang-banger who is sitting across the street. They won't invite the neighborhood kids to Sunday school, or tell that wino about God who loves him.

1965 started out with a bang. Almost every weekend there seemed to be a quarter party going on somewhere. Quarter parties were house parties where people were charged a quarter to get in. Some people called them blue light parties. They were also known as rent parties. Most of the time, the parties were held in the court way building across the street from my house. I was not allowed in that building because one day, some boys were playing with a gun and accidentally killed a girl in there. I went anyway. That was where Vivian and Elaine lived. Vivian lived on the first floor. Some parties were in her apartment, but most of them were upstairs in Elaine's apartment, where the girl was killed. Both of their mothers were single parents that worked a lot. So that was our hangout.

We started a social club called, "The Mack Men." We were not a gang, just a group of guys from the neighborhood that partied, played ball, and hung out together.

There was a group of guys from another neighborhood that would sometimes try to crash the parties and start trouble. They were part of Fat Nash's gang. One night, some of them came in and started a fight, so we all went outside. Butch was Betty Jean's cousin from the south side. He was bigger than the rest of us, and the only one with any gang fighting experience. So he stepped forward and challenged Saul, who was their captain. But Saul said he wasn't going to waste his time fighting a chump like Butch. So he called one of his boys, Clint, to do the fighting. Butch said he was not going to fight a chump like Clint. He told Clint to pick someone in our group that he wanted to fight. Clint picked me.

Clint was a big, black, corn bread eating, country boy. He was almost a foot taller than I was and he out weighed me by about thirty pounds, but I didn't care. I thought I was Cassius Clay (that was before he changed his name to Muhammad Ali). Besides that, the beer and whiskey I had been drinking at the party gave me all of the confidence I needed. I started dancing around and throwing jabs like I had seen Ali do on TV. I kept dancing in and jabbing him and then dancing back before he could hit me. Everyone was cheering me on and saying, "Go Bub, go." Then the whiskey started talking to me. It said, "Grab him and body slam him." I moved in and grabbed Clint around his waist and tried to pick him up.

When I woke up---I was in my bathroom lying on the floor and someone was putting cold water and wet towels on my face. I asked somebody what had happened. They kept asking me why I grabbed Clint. The whiskey told me to do it.

CHAPTER 1 - The Call

The following Friday night, Vivian had another party. I was dancing with Betty Jean when someone said that Saul and Clint were outside. I wanted a rematch with Clint, so we went outside. Butch and Chucky told me not to grab him this time. But before we started fighting, someone pulled a gun and started shooting. Although the person with the gun was not one of us, he was at the party with us. Eventually, word got back to Fat Nash that we had shot at some of his boys.

Everybody split up and went their separate ways. Chucky and Fuzzy went around the corner with Betty Jean and me to her house on Roosevelt Road. After we stayed there for a while, Fuzzy went across the street to his house. Chucky was able to get home by going through the alley, so he left too. I stayed a little while longer and was just about to leave when the phone rang. It was Chucky. He told me not to try to go home. He lived across the street from me, and could see my house from his front window. He told me that Fat Nash and some of his boys were sitting on my front porch waiting for me. I ended up staying at Betty Jean's all night, hoping her mother didn't wake up.

I didn't go to sleep at all that night. I spent the whole night pacing the floor and trying to figure out how I was going to get into my house without Fat Nash or my father catching me. Dad didn't play that staying-out-all-night stuff. Fat Nash was bad, but dad was badder. I found that out a few weeks earlier when I thought I was big enough to challenge him on his rules about where I could and could not go.

Ralph had gotten angry with me one day and told dad that I had been hanging out in Vivian and Elaine's building. I made a big mistake by telling my father that I could go wherever I wanted. But it was a bigger mistake to tell him that while I was standing at the top of the stairs. I realized that when I found myself lying at the bottom of those stairs in a lot of pain.

I called Chucky and asked him to look out of his window and see if the coast was clear. He said it was, so I headed home. It was about 6:00 in the morning. The whole time I was walking down Christiana, I was praying that I got home without Fat Nash's boys seeing me. I made it. Then I started praying that I could get into the house without my father hearing me. I made that too. As I was taking off my clothes, dad woke up. When he came into my room, I acted like I had just woken up and was putting my clothes on. He asked me what time I had gotten in last night. I told him I was home before my curfew. He said, "Good. Since you're up, go outside and water the grass."

The last thing I wanted to do was go back outside and possibly run into Fat Nash but I figured I had two choices. One, I could tell my father the truth, which included me being in Vivian and Elaine's building again. (The same building that got me knocked down the stairs.) Or two, I could go outside and water the lawn.

While I was watering the lawn, I kept looking up and down the street for Fat Nash and his boys. I was praying that they had gone home. I was about halfway finished when I heard something. When I turned around, there was Fat Nash, Saul, Clint, and two other guys. They had come through the gangway next to my house. I tried to tell them that I had nothing to do with the shooting, but they didn't want to hear it.

They were taking me toward the gangway that leads to the alley when Nelson, the neighborhood preacher, came out of nowhere. Boy was I glad to see him. They told him what my friends and I had done. Nelson asked them to just forget about it and let me go. Because of the respect that Fat Nash had for Nelson, they let me go.

Oh! I forgot to mention something. Fat Nash had a big brother, known as Big Nash. Their mother was a Pentecostal Evangelist.

After that incident, Nelson started recruiting some of the neighborhood boys for a basketball team. We had all grown up playing baseball, basketball, and football in the alley behind Christiana. We called the alley, "Christiana Stadium." We named the team, "The Harlem Browns," and sold chicken dinners to buy our uniforms. In order to be on the team we had to attend Bible study classes at Nelson's house. Most of the time his wife, Velma, was the teacher.

We had some pretty good players on our team. Besides Butch and Gip, there was Punchy, who played guard for Cregier High, Jerry, and Joe. However, the basketball team didn't last very long. We played in only a couple of tournaments. Some of the guys didn't like the Bible study part, but I did. Although I had grown up in church, the only parts of the Bible I had ever read were John 3:16 and the 23rd Psalm. I didn't know that the Bible was so exciting. I went home and started reading the Gospel of Matthew. I got so caught up in reading about the life of Jesus Christ, I couldn't put in down. I couldn't wait to get home everyday to see what happened next. I cried when I read about how they crucified Him and rejoiced when I read about His glorious resurrection.

I knew that it was time for me to change the way I was living. It was like the time my mother caught Ralph and I cursing. I was eleven or twelve years old at the time. A group named, "The Coasters" had recorded a song called "Charlie Brown." There was a different version of the song that was going around school. In that version, some of the words were changed and there were a lot of curse words being used. One night when our parents weren't home, Ralph and I were singing the school version of Charlie Brown, curse words and all. We were singing so loud and having so much fun, we didn't hear our mother come in, but unfortunately she heard us. Before we knew anything, she was lighting into our behinds with an ironing cord. While she was whipping us, she made us keep singing, Charlie Brown. After that night, I never wanted to hear Charlie Brown again. As a matter of fact, every time it came on the radio, I changed the station.

That is what we all must learn to do. Change the station. If it is your friends that are getting you into trouble and making you sin against God, change the station. Stay away from those friends. If it is the places that you go that bring on temptations, change the station. Don't go to those places. There might be something or someone that you are holding onto that is causing you to stumble. You know what you've got to do. Change the station.

I got down on my knees and begged God to forgive me for all of my sins. I will never forget how close I felt to God that night. My whole life was changed. I felt like I was a different person. I wanted to know more and more about Jesus. I started reading the book of Mark to see what happened next. To my surprise, much of it was the same as what was in Matthew. I read it anyway. But when I got to the part where they were going to crucify Him, I had to stop reading. I couldn't go through that again. It was just too painful. Imagine how painful it was for Him.

Some of the boys and girls in the neighborhood continued studying the Bible with Nelson and Velma. We joined the Galatians Missionary Baptist Church, a small storefront church on 15th and Millard. The pastor was a young, 24 year old preaching machine named Rev. Joe Jones. He was short, and he stomped when he preached. He built a little step behind the pulpit. That way, he could step up on it and lean over the pulpit when he preached.

He was a good singer too. Before he was a pastor, he sang with Nelson and Velma as part of the Holloway Community Singers. Although I wasn't much of a singer, I was in the choir. So was everybody else for that matter. There were about twenty members in the church, and fifteen of us were in the choir. Nelson was the director. I never led any songs. I just stood in the back and tried to blend in with everyone else. Rev. Jones, Velma, or Stean, another girl from Christiana, led most of the songs. Stean and her sister, Gloria, had grown up in the Pentecostal church. Gloria was Betty Jean's best friend and was part of the reason we were together.

One day, someone told me that my grandfather had fallen down the stairs on our front porch. He lived on the first floor of our building. I tried to help him up but he wasn't responding so I ran inside and called an ambulance. (There was no 911 at that time) The person that answered the phone asked me if I had any money to pay for the ambulance service. When I told him I didn't, he said I had to call the fire department. When they arrived, they took my grandfather to the hospital. He died anyway.

I really hated to see him go because he had been such a big part of my life. He was the one who walked me to and from school when I was a child. I also remember going to the Jack's Foxhole tavern with him and sitting on the bar stool next to his. I drank milk while he drank "something else." But that was our little secret. What I remember most about him was that he always dressed up. Despite him being retired, he wore a suit and tie everyday. Now he is gone. We buried him next to my grandmother who passed about a year or so before him.

That summer we had a weeklong revival at the church. The preacher was Elder James Kelly, pastor of the St. John Missionary Baptist Church on Gladys Avenue. Elder Kelly had a reputation of being a Holy Ghost filled Baptist preacher, and boy could he preach. I didn't know why he was called "Elder" instead of "Reverend," like all of the other preachers. Some people said he had come out of the Pentecostal church. Others said he wasn't a real Baptist. There was definitely something different about him. He had something that most preachers I had known did not have. I didn't know what it was, but I wanted it too.

I started preaching in our kitchen again, but Ralph had outgrown me, so I couldn't make him sit and listen to me anymore. Preaching was in me. The desire was getting stronger and stronger. I felt like the prophet Jeremiah. The word of God was like fire, shut up in my bones.

In September, school started back, and I started my junior year of high school. I was sitting in the back of the bus on my way home from school one day. The bus was full of people that were laughing and talking. I leaned back in my seat and closed my eyes, I could see myself preaching. I was just preaching, and preaching, and preaching. Before I realized it, I had missed my stop. I stayed on the bus and went to my aunt's house. She was a pastor in an African Methodist Episcopal Church named "Coston Chapel." Her name was Rev. Armie Rayford, but we called her Auntee. She had left the Baptist church years earlier because they did not recognize women as preachers, but the Methodist church did.

I told her what had happened on the bus and of my unquenchable desire to preach. I asked her if God was calling me to preach. She told me that He could be. She suggested I go home and pray some more. I went home and talked to my father about it.

Oh! I forgot to mention something. My father was a preacher too. He had accepted his call to the ministry late in his life. He had run from God for a long time. During most of my life, he had been an alcoholic like my grandfather, my uncles, and most of my family.

He was glad to hear that I was praying about my call. He prayed with me that the Lord would make clear to me what He wanted me to do. After praying for a few days, I realized that God had called me to preach His word a long time ago. I was ready to accept the call.

The next day, I talked to Rev. Jones about everything. After he was satisfied that I was sure of my call, he set a date for my trial sermon. December 5, 1965. That was almost three months away. I guess he was giving me plenty of time to either prepare or to change my mind. When I told Betty Jean about it, she said she had seen it coming and was happy about it too. After a while, word started spreading up and down Christiana that, "Bub is a preacher." Fuzzy and Chucky started teasing me and calling me, "Rev. Bub." I didn't care. I was sixteen years old, and had finally gotten the call that I had been waiting for since I was nine. I was going to be a preacher.

CHAPTER TWO

The Preacher

My trial sermon was about Daniel in the Lion's Den. Most of my family and friends were there. Gip was there too. I was surprised to see him because he was leaving for the Marines early the next morning. He had signed up to go to Vietnam on the buddy plan with Cy (Short for Cyclopes). We called him Cyclopes because he was so tall. But Cy failed his physical exam, so Gip went to Nam alone. He was the first of my friends to go, but he would not be the last. Butch would soon follow.

My sermon didn't go quite like I thought it would. I was under the impression that when I started talking, at some point, the Holy Spirit would take over and my voice would change and I would "tune up" and "hoop" all over the pulpit like I had seen other preachers do. It didn't happen. When I got to the end of the sermon nothing had changed. I sat down thinking that I knew how Jesus felt when He said, "My God, My God, why have you forsaken me?"

At the end of the program, Rev. Jones congratulated me and presented me with a certificate of license to preach the gospel in the Baptist church. Everyone came up to me, shaking my hand and telling me how well I had done. I started thinking that maybe I hadn't done so badly after all. But I still wasn't satisfied. I wanted to do better, much better. They raised an offering for me, but I gave it to the church like I had seen some other preachers do. When Nelson found out what I had done, he was very angry because he was counting on getting some of the money.

I quit school and got a job as a bus boy at a big, fancy, north side restaurant. The pay was $1.00 per hour. The manager asked me if I had any experience. I told him I had worked as a bus boy at Dave's restaurant. I didn't even know what a bus boy was. And Dave's wasn't really a restaurant. It was more like a neighborhood deli where school kids and area workers went for lunch. I had never worked there, but my friends and I ate there a lot. They had the best hot dogs and polish sausages around, besides Maxwell Street, known as "Jew Town."

I found out that bus boys cleaned the tables after the customers left. I also learned that the customers left money on the tables for tips. I thought the tips were left for me because I was the one that was cleaning up their mess. At Dave's, we always had to clean our own tables, like the fast food places today.

One afternoon, during lunch hour, I was really racking up a lot of money in tips. I had only been working for about four or five hours and my apron pockets were full of money. I loved that job. But when I looked around, I saw a waitress picking up the tip from one of the tables. I thought she was stealing my money. Then I saw another waitress picking up the tips. I was getting angry. I decided to go around to all of the tables and pick up the tips, then go back and clean the tables.

I was doing fine, until the manager came up to me. He asked me if I had been taking the tips from the tables. I said, "Yeah. And I want to report those waitresses. Some of them were stealing my money before I could get to it." He said, "That is not your money, it's theirs. I thought you said you did this before." I told him that we did things differently at the other restaurant.

He took all of the money I had in my apron and said if I picked up any more tips, he would not only fire me, but he would have me arrested for theft. I didn't think that was fair. I was doing all of the work. All they were doing was bringing out some food. I didn't like that job anymore. I stayed there for about a week, and then I got a job as a dishwasher at The International House of Pancakes. Now they are known as "IHOP."

Rev. Jones already had an assistant pastor, Rev. Robinson, so I didn't get a chance to preach very much, but that didn't bother me. I started preaching at some of my friend's homes, in their living rooms. I still sang with the choir, and I learned a lot from Rev. Jones. I loved to listen to him preach each Sunday. Just before his sermon he would always sing a solo. Usually, it was either "Poor Pilgrim of Sorrow" or "I Must Tell Jesus." I really loved Rev. Jones.

A few months later, Galatians Missionary Baptist Church, like so many other churches, split. When a church that small splits, there's not much left. I wish I would have stayed there with Rev. Jones, but after the split there were only five members left and two of them were preachers. I didn't think there was room enough for three. After checking out a few other churches, I decided to join the Greater Mt. Calvary Missionary Baptist Church on Roosevelt Road near St. Louis Ave. The pastor was my cousin, Rev. Edicott Ivy. He was about 20 years older than I was, and a powerful preacher. He had two brothers, Lee Howard and William Ivy, who were also pastors.

I got a nice job at Sears' corporate offices, working as a messenger making $70.00 a week. It was during that time that I got the news that my cousin, Junior Hawkins, who we called Hawk, had been killed in an automobile accident. He lived in St. Louis, where most of my mother's side of the family lived. I really loved Hawk, so I decided to fly in for the funeral. It was my first time flying. I think it took the taxicab longer to get to the airport than it took the plane to get to St. Louis.

There were two experiences that happened during that trip that I will never forget. The first one was my getting to know my Uncle Archie. We sat around talking for hours and he told me story after story. I started using some of those stories in many of my sermons. It had gotten to the point where people expected me to end my sermons with a story (I still use them today). Although I have added hundreds of stories to my repertoire, it all started with Uncle Archie.

The second incident was very painful for me. My mother and her sister, my Aunt Jessie, were talking just before leaving for the funeral. Aunt Jessie was Hawk's mother, and she was crying uncontrollably. She said, "Mary, why did God have to take my son? I only have one son. Why did he have to take my only son? You have two sons. Why didn't He take Bub?"

She didn't say, "Why didn't He take one of your sons." She named me. That statement hit me like a ton of bricks. How could she say that? I think what hurt me even more was the fact that my mother didn't defend me. They didn't see me standing there, so they never knew that I heard. I vowed that I would never go back to St. Louis again.

In all fairness to Aunt Jessie, she didn't know me. She knew and loved Ralph because he had spent the first four years of his life in St. Louis with my mother and her side of the family because of my parent's separation. Therefore, he was the favorite of everyone there. Likewise, I lived in Chicago with my father and his side of the family, so I was the favorite there.

I wish I had tried to protect Ralph more from the mistreatment he endured from some of our family members in Chicago. Some of them thought Ralph was not really my father's son because he was born in St. Louis. They treated him like a stepchild. I think that really had a lasting effect on him. He was my little brother and I was supposed to look out for him. Years later, after Aunt Jessie and I got to know each other, we became very close. She was really a wonderful person.

After the funeral, I was glad to get back to Chicago and to my church. I learned a lot under Rev. Ivy. He was the one who taught me what the role of a preacher was and how I was to act, both in and out of the pulpit. He called it "Pulpit Etiquette." I was ordained under him. That was a very scary experience. I was 17 years old and was surrounded by a group of older pastors who were questioning me about the Articles of Faith and the Baptist Doctrine. I had thought that since Rev. Ivy was my cousin, he would go easy on me. I was wrong. To him, there was no favoritism as far as the ministry was concerned. He felt that if he let me slide by being unprepared, he would be hurting me more than helping me.

I acted as one of his assistants for a while but I was coming more and more under the influence of Nelson, who I later found out was responsible for the split of Galatians Missionary Baptist Church. He was able to convince a lot of the young people, including myself, that the Baptist church was not as holy as it should be. So we left the Baptist denomination in search of "the perfect church."

During our search, we went through a few denominational and non-denominational churches. Eventually we stopped going to other churches. We became our own church. That was when Nelson said that God told him that I was a Bishop. So at age 18, I became, "Bishop Barr." Nelson was the prophet and faith healer. Sometimes we would go downtown to the A.A. Allen Crusades whenever he was in town. Allen was a famous faith healer. We started conducting crusades around town ourselves. I would preach, and Nelson would lay hands on people. The name of our ministry was, *"World Wide Wonders and Miracles Soul Saving Revivals."*

It was during that time that Nelson started convincing some people in our group to quit school. He told us that neither Jesus nor the Apostles went to school. What he really wanted was for us to get jobs so we could give him our tithes (the 10% of our income that belongs to God). Sometimes he wasn't satisfied with the 10%. He would tell each of us how much of our paychecks God had told him to tell us to give.

He had a way of using the Bible to prove his point. What none of us knew at the time was, he would take a verse or two from the Bible, and use it out of context so it would suit his purpose. That was how he was able to turn some of us against our parents, our friends, and other family members. We didn't know it at the time, but we were a cult.

Nelson moved off of Christiana and into a large apartment on Roosevelt Road near Pulaski Avenue. I left home and moved in with them. I had a room with his sons and his nephew, Larry. Most of our revivals lasted anywhere from three days to a week. In the summer of 1967, we went to Detroit for a revival that was scheduled to last two weeks. I was excited about the prospect of preaching in other cities the way Billy Graham and A.A. Allen did.

The revival was held at Faith Tabernacle, a non-denominational church in Highland Park, Michigan, a section of Detroit. The pastor was Rev. Morris Thomas, Sr., a former Methodist pastor. His wife, Betty, was very beautiful and one of the nicest people I had ever met. She played piano at the church. Ronnie, our van driver, and I were guests at their home while we were there.

We met many nice people and had a really good time. Rev. Thomas was a very wise man and he was able to see right through Nelson. Needless to say, he did not like what he saw. Before we left Detroit, he called me off to the side and said, "Watch yourself Rev. Barr, Brown is not what you think he is."

When the revival was over, we were ready to head back to Chicago. As we were leaving, a riot was breaking out. We were not able to get any gas for the journey because all of the stations were closing. When we were on Interstate 94, leaving Detroit, all I saw was a lot of smoke and flames; It looked like a war zone. I remember saying a prayer for Rev. Thomas, the people at Faith Tabernacle, and the city of Detroit.

When we got back to Chicago, I got a job at the Shell Oil Company's corporate offices downtown at 10 South Riverside Plaza. Velma had had another baby so they got Betty Jean to move into the house and take care of him. She slept on a rollaway bed in the kitchen.

Whenever anyone would challenge Nelson, he would prophesy that something bad was going to happen to them, trying to frighten them and the others. You must remember, we were all still kids. Calvin was his favorite target because he was the oldest and he spoke his mind most of the time. Nelson would try to use Calvin's wife, Tiny, to keep him in check but she wasn't very successful, so he tried to break them up. (I heard he eventually did.) There were two married couples in our group. Calvin and Tiny was one couple and Rudolph and Willa were the other. Willa and Tiny were cousins. Betty Jean and I was the only other couple and Nelson was always trying to break us up too but we had been together for three years.

In September of that year, Nelson, Velma, (who was now called, "Mother Superior,") and some of the others, went to New York for a revival. I didn't want to go with them that time because I was starting to see Nelson for what he was, a con man. I started thinking about some of the things I had seen him do that was not right or, at the very least, were questionable. Like the time we were all in a dark room and he tried to convince us that he had just turned a bowl of water into wine. But he wouldn't let anyone turn the lights on so we could have a better look. Or the time he told us to tell our parents and everyone on Christiana that he had been shot.

Although I was his right hand man, I was getting to the point where I didn't want to be around him anymore. Besides, I didn't want to leave Betty Jean to go to New York. While they were gone, Betty let me know that she was tired of the way things were going too. She was ready for us to get married and be on our own. I should have listened to her.

How could I just walk out on someone who had done so much for me? He was the one that saved me from Fat Nash and his boys. He was the one who taught me the Bible (or so I thought), and had gotten me into church. If it had not been for him, I probably would not have even been a preacher. Even though I didn't agree with some of the things he was doing, I still felt a certain degree of loyalty toward him.

When they got back from New York, I told Nelson that Betty Jean and I were going to get married and we were leaving. He didn't want me to leave because I was the reason most of the people from Christiana had hooked up with him in the first place. They had grown up with me. They knew me. They trusted me. He thought if I left, some of them would go with me and I would split his church the same way he had split Galatians Baptist church under Rev. Jones. I didn't know this at the time, but he didn't want Betty Jean to leave because, even though he was married, he wanted her for himself. I agreed to wait a while before leaving. That was a mistake that cost me dearly.

One morning, as I was getting ready for work, everyone else in the house was asleep. I went into the kitchen to get something and I saw Betty Jean lying in the rollaway bed, sleeping. I looked at her for a while. She looked so beautiful. I remember thinking how glad I would be when we were finally married and moved out on our own. I went over to her and started caressing her face. I started reminiscing and thinking about all of the good times we had had together.

But then my mind started going in another direction. When I said earlier that she was my very first love, I meant it in more ways than one. Before long, I wasn't just touching her face. My hands were all over her. I started unbuttoning her pajamas and touching her where I should not have. Before I knew it, I had pulled my pants down and my penis out. I started rubbing it against her. I thank God I came to myself and stopped before I did something I would have regretted. Betty and I had made love many times, but that was before we came to Christ. Although I wanted her body very badly, I couldn't do that to her. I loved her too much. So I pulled my pants up, put the blanket back over her and left.

The guilt of what I had done, and almost had done, was eating at me. I didn't go to work that day. I went to the movies instead. It was the first time I had been to the movies in years. Nelson believed going to the movies was a sin. The movie that was playing was, "Divorce, American Style" staring Dick Van Dyke. It was about a man who was planning to cheat on his wife. His friend, a master cheater, was telling him how to get away with it. He told him to deny everything. Even if he was caught in the act, still deny it. His words were, "deny, deny, deny."

That was what I decided to do when I got home. Deny everything. I figured that Betty Jean would know that I had been messing with her. She had to. I had left her pajamas undone. I would just say that it wasn't me, but I couldn't do that. I couldn't lie to her. I loved her. I decided to tell her the truth and ask her to forgive me. I decided it was time for us to get married and leave, no matter what Nelson said. I was eighteen years old and Betty Jean was nineteen. We were grown.

But when I got home, everything had changed. Betty Jean was in the back room with Velma, and Nelson accused me of raping her. What made it worse was, he had convinced Betty Jean and everyone else in our church that I had raped her too. What happened was, when Betty Jean woke up and found her pajamas in disarray, she figured someone had been messing with her, but she didn't know it was me. So she told Velma, who told Nelson. And together, they were able to convince her that I had raped her while she was asleep.

After that, I was pretty much ostracized from the group. I had lost the respect of everyone. What hurt most was I lost Betty Jean, the girl I loved. I had given Nelson just what he wanted. He had won. I figured it was time for me to go. I just wished I had done it sooner, when Betty Jean wanted us to leave.

I felt like that old lady who was in the commercial. I had fallen, and I couldn't get up. I thought about the time, when I was seven years old. I was playing outside in front of my house when a girl that was riding a bicycle knocked me down and ran me over. I kept trying to get up, but couldn't. I was in a lot of pain. What I didn't know was, my leg was broken. I remembered that my father was in the house, and he had the window open so he could hear me if I called him. So I started yelling, "Daddy, Daddy." Before I knew it, he had reached down and picked me up. Sometimes even the strongest Christians fall. But we've got to remember that our Father is in Heaven and has the window open so He can hear us. And when we do, He will reach down and pick us up. *If we confess our sins, He is faithful and just to forgive us our sins, and to cleanse us from all unrighteousness. (1 John 1:9)*

That Friday evening after work, I went back home. My mother and father were glad to see me, and so was Ralph. I hadn't seen them for more than a year. The next day my mother cooked a big meal and my father and I hung out all day. Early Sunday morning the phone rang. It was Nelson. He and Calvin had gone to Detroit for another revival. He said they really needed my help, and asked if I could come there. I was going to church with my father, so I told him that I would call him back.

I liked Detroit, so I decided to go. I caught a flight that got me there in time for the revival that night. I got there at about 5:00 pm and called Nelson to let him know I was at the airport. He said they would pick me up before they went to the church, so I waited, and waited, and waited. Finally at about 10:00 PM I was so angry I started walking to Detroit. Someone had told me that Detroit was about 40 miles from the airport, but I didn't care about the distance until I started walking. I was a city boy and there I was walking through the country, at night. I wasn't prepared for what I saw, or couldn't see. I was used to seeing streetlights but there were none. It was dark, real dark. It was also cold and scary.

When I got to the next town, I called Rev. Thomas and he came and got me. While we were riding, I told him what had happened. When we got to his house he asked me what I planned to do. I told him I would decide the next day. He went upstairs to bed and I let the couch out and lay down. Before I went to sleep, the doorbell rang. It was Nelson. He apologized for not picking me up and asked me to rejoin them because they couldn't do the revivals without me. Against my better judgment, I went back with them. When I got to Chicago, I went back to Nelson's, but it just wasn't the same. I wasn't comfortable there anymore.

When I went to work one day, my boss called me into his office. He had some papers on his desk that I later found out were telephone bills for my phone extension. After watching the St. Louis Cardinals in the 1967 World Series, I wanted to play professional baseball. So I had been calling some of the major league franchises around the country, trying to get one of them to let me try out for their team. The calls would have been free if I had used the company's Watts line. That was the phone line we were supposed to use when making business related long distance calls but it was hard to get through on the Watts line sometimes and I was impatient. So I used the regular line.

He told me that most of the numbers I had called were not in the company's directory. He asked me if they were personal or business calls. I told him that some of them were personal and some were business. I thought he would let it go at that, but he looked at his list and started calling off cities and phone numbers. After each one, he asked if it was business or personal. He said, "St. Louis," I said, "personal," He said, "Los Angeles," I said "personal," He said, Detroit," I said, "personal" He named a few more cities and I said personal to all of them. I decided that I had confessed to enough of the calls, so when he said, "New York," I said, "I don't know. I think that one was business." I thought he was going to leave it at that and go on to the next number. But instead he said, "Ok. Let's just dial the number and see who answers." Using the Watts line, he dialed the number. He sat there holding the phone, waiting for someone on the other end to answer. All of a sudden he jumped up and shouted, "YANKEE STADIUM." He hung up the phone and looked at me in anger and disbelief. I cleared my throat and said, "personal."

He didn't fire me, but he said he would be watching the phone bills closely. And if there were any more calls like that, I would be history. But what he didn't know was that there were more calls, lots of them. They would be on the next bill so I knew I was going to have to quit before that bill came.

It turned out that all of the calls were not in vain. The Los Angeles Dodgers had agreed to let me try out for their winter ball club but I would have to pay my own expenses, such as travel, lodging, and food until I made the team (if I made the team). I called Greyhound and discovered that a one-way ticket from Chicago to Los Angeles was $52.00. I decided to go.

I quit my job, packed my clothes, and the next day I went to the bus station. But while I was there, I started thinking. I had two weeks pay, which was about $160.00. When I got to L.A. I would probably have less than 100.00 left. I would have to get a room and buy food. What if I didn't make the team?

Oh! I forgot to mention something. I had never played baseball in my life. I had played a lot of softball, but I had never played league ball. I changed my mind about going to Los Angeles. I asked the ticket agent where the next bus was going. He said it was going to Cleveland. I bought a one-way ticket.

When I arrived in Cleveland, I got a room at the West Side YMCA. It was a nice, clean place and I liked it. I got a job as a telemarketer; although I don't think they were called that in 1967. I hated that job. On my first day there, I went to lunch and never returned. I called Rev. Thomas and a few other people I had met when I was in Detroit. One of them, a young lady named Dee Dee, invited me to have Thanksgiving dinner with her family. I had met her during the revival that summer. So two weeks after leaving Chicago, I was on a Greyhound bus again. This time I was on my way to Detroit, Michigan.

I had one of the best Thanksgivings I'd had in a long time. I spent time with Rev. Thomas and his family, and I went out with Dee Dee. I was trying to forget about Betty Jean. During that time, Rev. Thomas let me know that he needed help at his church. His assistant, Rev. Pearson, had gone to another church. He told me that he needed an assistant pastor, and if I wanted to move to Detroit, I was welcomed to stay at his house until I got on my feet. I think he and Sister Thomas were kind of concerned about me being in Cleveland by myself. So, the day after Thanksgiving, I went back to Cleveland, packed my clothes, and caught a bus back to Detroit.

I moved in with Rev. Thomas and his family in Highland Park on Doris Avenue. Rev. Thomas was a mail carrier and his wife, Betty, worked for the telephone company. They had four children: Morris Jr., Ricky, Tony, and Lisa who all made me feel like I was part of the family. Every Sunday morning, Sister Thomas would cook a big breakfast before we all went to church. Morris Jr.

didn't have to go because he was grown. Ricky didn't want to go, but he had no choice since he was still a teenager.

Faith Tabernacle was a small storefront church. There was no choir, so we would sing congregational songs and have testimony service before Rev. Thomas preached. My favorite singer was a sister named Justine. We called her, "Sister So Good," because that was the name of the song she always sang, "So good." After the sermon, people would line up for prayer and he would lay hands on them and pray for them. Rev. Thomas preached every Sunday morning, and I preached every Sunday night. I had developed a preaching style like Rev. Jones. I would stomp my foot, and as my father used to say, "rare back and holler."

One night, I decided to do like Rev. Jones and sing "Poor Pilgrim of Sorrow" just before I preached. It was not a pretty sight. Or should I say, it was not a pretty sound. I had planned to sing a cappella (without any music) but Sister Thomas didn't know that and she started playing along with me. First of all, Sister Thomas was not the greatest pianist. She had many gifts, but playing the piano was not one of them. She couldn't find the key that I was trying to sing in, probably because there was no such key. Like I said, it was not a pretty sight. The piano was not her gift, and singing wasn't mine. That was the last time I ever tried to sing in church (or in public at all for that matter).

I got a job at Niesner Brothers, a five and ten cents store, as an Assistant Manager Trainee. It was a nice job and it was in walking distance from home, and one block from the church. The store was closed on Sundays so it didn't interfere with worship services. I had a key to the church, so I would go there on my lunch hour and preach to the empty pews. Sometimes people that were passing by heard me preaching and came in, thinking there was a worship service going on.

I was working in the stock room one day in the early part of 1968 when one of the ladies came in and told me that someone was looking for me. I went out to the sales floor to see who it was. It was Nelson. He tried to talk me into going back to Chicago and helping him again. I told him no, I was happy where I was. Then he said, "You could at least send us your tithes." I couldn't believe he said that. I said, "I pay my tithes at my church." Then I turned around and walked back into the stock room.

There was a young lady at Niesner's that I couldn't help noticing. Her name was Charlotte. She was very beautiful, and had a smile that could brighten up the darkest room. She was also very shy. We talked a lot, and occasionally had lunch together. I could tell that there was something very special about Charlotte.

One day while we were having lunch, she told me that she was pregnant. It had happened before we met and the would-be father was not in her life, nor was he in the picture. I wasn't going to judge her. It was only by the grace of God that I didn't have any children myself. I had been sexually active since I was fifteen. Besides, I was starting to feel like she was the one I wanted to spend the rest of my life with. Although we had never had sex, I would have married her and told everyone that the baby was mine. Just as we were really getting to know each other, she disappeared. For weeks I called her house and left messages, but she never returned my calls. Sister Thomas saw how bad I was hurting, and tried her best to comfort me. In just over a year I had lost two women that I had really cared about; first Betty Jean, and now Charlotte.

I left Neisner's and was hired at F. W. Woolworth's for their management-training program. It was a four-year program designed to teach trainees every job in the store from the stock room, to the sales floor, to the office. I was assigned to a large, two level store located on Woodward and Grand Boulevard, down the street from Motown Record Studios. I was blessed because that store was closed on Sundays too. Since I had stock room experience at Niesner's, I was put on the sales floor in charge of the entire lower level. I felt like my life was finally coming together. I had a career with a good company, and I was coming into my own as a preacher of the gospel.

During the first week in April, I was preaching my first revival since leaving Nelson. It was at a very large, all white church that once was a movie theater. They had wanted Rev. Thomas, but he was not available because there was a revival going on at our church, so he asked if I could go instead. I was kind of nervous because I had never preached to an all white congregation before, and I didn't know how they would react to my stomping and hollering, but it went very well.

Each night I would catch the bus after leaving work and get to the church shortly after the services began. Everything was going great and I was enjoying being in revival again. I was getting to know a lot of the people and the attendance grew each night.

One night, I missed my bus so I got to the church later than usual. After walking in, I sensed there was something wrong. While I was walking down the aisle toward the stage, the pastor's son tried to get my attention. I looked at him, and he was saying something and pointing to the side of his head as if his hand was a gun. I was already late, so I kept walking. When I got to my seat I heard the pastor say that Dr. Martin Luther King Jr. had been assassinated. I continued and preached that night, but we closed out the revival after that.

The bus ride home was very long. I just sat there on that bus thinking about the time my father had taken me to see Dr. King at Soldier's Field in Chicago when I was 12 or 13 years old. I remember watching and listening to Dr. King speak that day and how it impacted my life. I also thought about the time that word had gotten around the neighborhood that he was at one of the slum apartments on Douglas Boulevard near Homan Avenue, and how my friends and I were running down Christiana, trying to see him. He was a hero to many people. Yes, it was a very long ride home.

When I got to work the next morning, there was a table set up at the front door with pictures of Dr. King in gold frames. Mr. Riley, the store manager, was standing there and apologizing to me for what had happened to Dr. King. To this day, I cannot understand how they were able to get all of those pictures to the stores so quickly.

Later that day, I saw a young black man trying to steal something from the store. I confronted him and told him that I didn't want to get him into any trouble, but he had to put the stuff back. He asked me how I could protect the white man's stuff after what they had done to Dr. King. He called me an Uncle Tom and said that I had better watch myself when I left the store because he was going to put the word out about me.

40

I didn't know whether to take him seriously or not, but I was concerned for my safety. Even more than that, I was hurt and angry that he had the audacity to call me an Uncle Tom just because I wouldn't let his stealing jeopardize my job. That was not what Dr. King was about. I didn't turn him in. I just told him to put the stuff back.

About a month later, I had just finished preaching at Faith Tabernacle when I saw a beautiful young lady sitting in the back of the church. After service, I went over and introduced myself. She said her name was Jeri (her real name was Jerzine but she didn't like it). Her mother and one of her sisters had attended the revival that Nelson and I had conducted the previous summer. Jeri's parents were strong Christians and two of the sweetest people you ever want to meet. They were members of Shiloh Church of God in Christ.

I don't know why, but I had been curious about the Church of God in Christ for some time. Maybe it was because they called their preachers Elders, and that was where Elder Kelly had come from. Or maybe I thought that it was my last hope of finding the "perfect" church.

Before I left Chicago, I remember walking down the street Sunday morning to the St. James Church of God in Christ. It was located on Roosevelt Road, in K-Town. The streets between Pulaski Ave. and Cicero Ave. were called K-Town because all of them, except one, began with the letter K. Trip Ave. was the exception. I arrived at 11:00 AM because that was the time most churches started. I found out their services didn't start until 1:00 PM, so I left.

Jeri and I started dating. On our first date, we went to a bowling alley that was near a club called, "The 20 Grand." It was my first time bowling, and it was a lot of fun. When we were leaving the bowling alley, I could hear the D.J. in the club playing the Temptations new record, "I Wish It Would Rain." It had been a long time since I'd heard the Temptations, or any other R&B singers for that matter. With Nelson, all of that stuff was a sin. As a matter of fact, almost everything was a sin. If it was fun, it was a sin.

THE HOODLUM PREACHER

Jeri had a cute little son, named Everett. Although "break dancing" didn't come out until the 1980's, Everett had it down pat way back in 1968. He was two years old, and when he had one of his temper tantrums, he would lie down on the floor, hold his breath, and spin around in circles.

Two of Jeri's sisters got married that summer. Lois, her eldest sister was first. She was my favorite. Her husband's name was Johnny. I really liked him. He had a great sense of humor and I thought they were the perfect couple. Evelyn was next. She was the prettiest. She married a guy named Dan who seemed to be pretty cool. Before long, Jeri and I were engaged. She was the sexiest of all of the sisters.

Rev. Thomas gave me an old car that needed a lot of work, but it still ran. It was my very first car, a 1959 Chevy Impala. The brakes were bad, the oil leaked, only one of the high beam headlights worked, and neither of the low beams did. Rev. Thomas told me to get my driver's license and have the necessary work done on the car before I drove it, but I was too impatient for that. I had my own car and I was going to drive it.

Oh! I forgot to mention something. I didn't know how to drive. No one in my immediate family ever had a car or knew how to drive, so I actually never learned. However, I was not going to let that stop me from driving my car.

One day, I was driving down a street named Davison, in Highland Park. I had never driven on that street before, but it seemed to be nice and peaceful. I was driving along, enjoying the sights, when all of a sudden, the sights changed. I was completely surrounded by a cars, and they were going fast, really fast. What I didn't know was, at some point with no warning at all, nice, peaceful Davison Avenue became the Davison Freeway. Although it is a relatively short freeway, it seemed like it was 50 miles to me. Cars were moving fast and I didn't know how to get off.

That's how Satan fools us sometimes. He gets us to the point where we become comfortable in our sins. He tricks us into thinking that those little sins we are committing are really no big deal. He tells us that God knows that we're not perfect but what we don't realize is that we are getting further and further out of God's will. We're just rolling along, enjoying ourselves and becoming more and more comfortable with what we are doing, until all of a sudden, we find ourselves on "Sin Freeway" and we don't know how to get off.

One day, I decided to drive to Jeri's house. When I got there I talked her into taking a ride with me. I was trying to impress her, but I think I ended up almost scaring her to death. After that, she and Lois taught me how to drive.

The brakes were starting to get worse. At first, there was a scrubbing sound. Then, they sounded like they were squealing. They were so loud, people walking down the streets turned and looked at me. Everyone told me to either get those brakes fixed or stop driving the car. So, I quit driving for a while.

On the fourth of July I was driving to Jeri's house. It was a beautiful day, and since it was a holiday there wasn't much traffic. I noticed that the brakes weren't scrubbing or squealing anymore. There was no noise at all. I was happy because I thought God had fixed my brakes. It was a miracle. I couldn't wait to get to Jeri's so I could tell her what God had done. I was going to show her, her parents, Rev. Thomas, and everybody else that they were wrong. I didn't have to get my brakes fixed. God had miraculously fixed them, or so I thought.

I was driving down Oakman Boulevard when the light up ahead turned red. When I stepped on the brakes, my foot went to the floor, but the car didn't stop. It didn't even slow down. My brakes were completely gone and I went right through the light.

I tried not to panic. I started driving into the curb trying to slow down. I looked ahead to the next intersection. The light was red and there were a lot of cars going by. I knew I had to stop the car before I got to the corner. I kept driving into the curb, but that wasn't helping. As I neared the intersection, I saw a big tree on my left. I had two choices. I could take my chances with the traffic, or I could drive into the tree. I braced myself and aimed for the tree.

When I hit the tree, my face hit the steering wheel and I bust my lip. I was a little dazed but I wasn't really hurt. Since I didn't have a driver's license, I decided to get out of the car and play it off by walking away like I was going for help. What I was really trying to do was to get away from the car before the police came. I reached for the door handle, but someone opened the door

43

for me. It was the police. I was trying to figure out where they came from. They must have been in the trunk.

One of them helped me out of the car and asked if I was okay. When I told him I was, He asked me if I had been drinking. I said, "No. I'm a preacher." Then he asked to see my driver's license. When I said I didn't have one, he told me to have a seat in the squad car. For the first time in my life, I was on my way to jail. If you read the introduction of this book, you know it wouldn't be my last.

I learned something else that day too. When you know there is something wrong, get it fixed. I'm not just talking about cars. There are a lot of people whose lives are broken. They see that things are getting worse, but they are not doing anything to improve their situation. They are waiting for God to step in and fix everything. What they don't realize is that God sometimes fixes things by opening the right doors, or giving us the resources we need, or placing certain people in our lives to guide us in the right direction.

I knew my brakes were bad. The more I drove, the louder the scrubbing became. It had gotten to the point that I hated stepping on the brakes because of all of the noise. I had the resources to fix the brakes and people who knew about cars kept trying to warn me, but I wouldn't listen. Instead of taking advantage of their wisdom and advice and using what God had already given me, I tried to turn God into an auto mechanic. As a result, my car was gone and I was on my way to jail.

I was in the lock-up for about three hours before Rev. Thomas got there with the $50.00 to bail me out. He gave me a lecture while we were riding home but I didn't mind. I had it coming. When we got home, I caught the bus to Jeri's house. I should have done that in the first place. I went to court a couple of months later and was given a fine. I just wanted to put all of that behind me and focus on my upcoming wedding.

Rev. Thomas tried to talk me out of getting married. I think he knew that I was "in lust," not in love. I think I was on a double rebound. I was still in love with Charlotte, and I hadn't forgotten about Betty Jean. Usually I listened to Rev. and Sister Thomas. They were like a father and mother to me and I often

44

sought their advice. My mother and father tried talking to me too, but I wasn't hearing anyone. This time, my mind was made up, and I was getting married before I lost Jeri too.

I spent a lot of time at Jeri's leading up to our wedding day. It was during that time, another one of my heroes, Senator Robert F. Kennedy, was gunned down while campaigning for the presidency. I watched the news reports with Jeri and her family at their house. We were all praying that Senator Kennedy would be all right. But apparently God had other plans. Bobby died just like his older brother, John, and Dr. King had, by an assassin's bullet.

About a week or so before my wedding, Sister Thomas called me to the phone. I noticed she had a strange look on her face. As she was handing me the phone, she said, "Remember, Rev. Barr, you're getting married next week." I was wondering what that was all about and quickly found out. It was Charlotte on the phone. When I heard her voice, all of the feelings I'd had for her were back.

Charlotte's mother had sent her to a home for pregnant girls. In those days, there was a stigma attached to young girls who had gotten pregnant out of wedlock. So, their parents would send them away until the baby was born and then put the baby up for adoption. Now that Charlotte was back, she called me, hoping I still felt the same about her. I did, but it was too late for us. I was getting married in less than two weeks. I came really close to calling the wedding off and asking Charlotte to marry me. If it had not been for Sister Thomas, I probably would have.

Jeri and I were married on August 17, 1968. We had a big church wedding and Rev. Thomas performed the ceremony. My mother came from Chicago along with Ralph, Butch, and my cousin Rose. Rose is like my big sister. She lived with us on Christiana during the early years of my life, and we have always been very close. She taught me everything, from how to play "hop scotch," to how to treat a lady. I was, however, kind of disappointed because my father didn't make it.

Jeri and I got an apartment somewhere on the west side of Detroit. I continued working at Woolworth's and she was a stay-at-home mom. It was around that time when Ben Taylor, a friend of mine, accepted his call to preach. Ben had recently joined Faith

45

Tabernacle and was a very good singer. When Ben preached his trial sermon, he lit the church up. I was really proud of him (and maybe a little jealous too). That was how I wanted my trial sermon to go. I didn't realize it at the time, but preachers that can sing use their singing voice at the end of their sermon when they hoop (tune-up). I didn't have a singing voice (I still don't), so I stomped my foot and hollered instead.

Ben started dating Ora, Dee Dee's older sister. Ora was a member of Faith Tabernacle too, and later became one of Jeri's best friends. Jeri went to church with me sometimes, but not as much as I would have liked. Sometimes we would visit other churches around Detroit when there were special programs going on. Jeri and her sisters were very good singers.

In October, after my 20th birthday, I decided it was time to go back to Chicago. So after talking it over with Jeri, I put in for a transfer. After saying our goodbyes to Jeri's family, Rev. Thomas and his family, the people at Faith Tabernacle, and everyone else, I was on a Greyhound bus again but this time I had my family with me.

When we got to Chicago, we temporarily moved in with my parents until our apartment was ready. It was the family building I had grown up in. The one I told you about in the opening chapter, 1230 S. Christiana. My mother, father, and Ralph lived on the second floor. The first floor, where my grandparents used to live, was rented out to Smitty and his wife, Ruth.

Ralph gave up his room for Jeri and me. He slept in, "The Bar." The Bar was a small room in the building next door to where my parents used to entertain their friends before my father became a preacher. It was furnished with a small bar with stools, a sofa bed, a card table, and chairs. When we were teenagers, that was the spot where we hung out with our friends. That was where most of the kids of Christiana lost their virginity, including Betty Jean and myself.

Woolworth's corporate office for the Chicago area was in Des Plaines, Illinois. I rode the train, so I got there about an hour early. Since I had some time to spare, I decided to find a place to get a cup of coffee. I was in luck. There was a Woolworth store with a lunch counter close by. I thought I would be able to talk with some of the employees about the company since they were so close to the offices. So, I went in and took a seat on one of the stools.

The store wasn't open yet, but the lunch counter was open for breakfast. After sitting there for almost ten minutes, I looked around trying to see what was taking the waitress so long to take my order. After all, there was only one other person sitting there, and he was already sipping his coffee.

When I looked around, I saw two waitresses standing at the end of the counter, smoking cigarettes and looking at me. I sat there a little longer, but it was apparent that they were not going to wait on me. I was getting very angry and my stubbornness started to come out. I just sat there until it was time for my appointment.

Oh! I forgot to mention something. Everyone in the store was white. And so was everyone in Des Plaines.

As I walked the two blocks to the corporate office building, I kept thinking about how I couldn't even get a cup of coffee in a store that was owned by the company that I worked for. I started thinking about Dr. King and all of the people who were involved in the civil rights movement in the south. I thought about the sit-ins, the marches, and the demonstrations they had gone through because they were being denied the basic rights and services to which we are all entitled.

So why couldn't I get a cup of coffee? I wasn't in the south. I wasn't in Alabama or Mississippi. I was right outside of Chicago, and I worked for that company. What I didn't know at the time was that the sit-ins took place at Woolworth's lunch counters.

My mind went back to the day after Dr. King was assassinated. I thought about the brother who had asked me, how I could protect the white man's stuff after what they had done to Dr. King. It seemed like I could still hear him calling me an Uncle Tom and telling me I had better watch myself. Suddenly his words had a different meaning.

I was assigned to the Woolworth store on Madison and Karlov, near Pulaski Ave. on the west side. It was smaller than the store in Detroit and a lot more dangerous. It was in a very bad neighborhood and all of the male employees, including

47

management, carried black jacks in their pockets. All of the employees were minorities, except the store manager. The store was opened on Sundays, but since Sundays were short days, (12 noon till 5 PM instead of 9 AM till 8 PM) Claude, another trainee, agreed to work my Sundays and I worked his Wednesdays.

I visited a few churches to see which one I might want to join. One Sunday, I went to the St. James Church of God in Christ. The pastor was Bishop Campbell. I didn't really know much about the Church of God in Christ (COGIC) denomination, but I liked that particular church and the people there. I didn't know why, but I felt that God was leading me there.

When I told Jeri that I was thinking about joining St. James, she hit the roof. She didn't want to have anything to do with the COGIC. I was surprised at that since it was her family's denomination. She let me know that she had no intention of joining that church, but that was where I felt led to be. Besides, she wasn't going to any of the churches with me anyway. So after talking with Bishop Campbell, I became a member of the St. James Church of God in Christ.

I soon became friends with Bishop Campbell's son, Elder Willie James Campbell. Most people called him W.J., but some of us called him Dub (short for, "W"). Elder Campbell was about a year or two older than I was, and boy could he preach. He was a younger version of Elder Kelly. There was another preacher that was in our circle, Elder Kennedy. We were like the three musketeers. We were always together. Whenever one of us was preaching somewhere, the other two always went to support him.

Most of the time, we were going to support Elder Campbell, because most pastors wanted him to preach for them, and he was quickly making a name for himself. There were many preachers who were jealous of Elder Campbell. They said that the only reason everyone was inviting him to preach was because his father was a bishop but I didn't believe that. I saw something in him. It was the same thing I had seen in Elder Kelly. I didn't know what it was, but I wanted it. They both preached with such power. I had not seen that in many preachers.

In January of 1969, Jeri and I finally moved into our apartment next door at 1234 S. Christiana. It was on the second floor over the bar. It was a large apartment with a living room, dining room, one bedroom, kitchen, and two walk-in closets. That was where my father's sister, "Auntee" and her husband, Uncle Ray, lived when Ralph and I were children. At that time, one of my father's other sisters, Aunt Ruth and her husband, Uncle Hebert, lived on the first floor next to the bar. That seemed like the perfect place for Uncle Hebert to live, next to the bar, because he was the neighborhood drunk. He was the Otis Campbell (from the Andy Griffith Show) of Christiana.

The first floor had been vacant for a long time. When we were teenagers, my friends and I used it for a clubhouse. We called it, "The Sweet Shop" because my father had used it for a candy store for a while. We had gotten that name from the Bowery Boys movies.

I was working long hours at Woolworth's during the week, and was at church all day on Sunday. I was starting to feel like Jeri and I were drifting apart. She seldom went to church. She spent a lot of time with my mother, who didn't go to church either.

Instead of working on our marriage, I spent more and more time hanging with Campbell, Kennedy, and the other young people from the church. We all had fun going downtown to restaurants, or just messing around together. I really wanted Jeri to go with me, but she seldom did. Sometimes I would talk to Bishop Campbell or his wife, Mother Campbell, about my failing marriage. They would pray with me and encourage me to hang in there.

We had been blessed with a car, a 1963 Plymouth. I was driving home from work one Saturday night when I decided to stop at a store on Roosevelt Road. When I walked out of the store I heard someone calling me. I looked around to see who it was. It was Nelson. We talked for a while and he asked me if I wanted to go by his house to see Velma and Betty Jean, who still lived with them. I wanted to see Betty Jean again so I went.

She was as beautiful as ever. Just seeing her again messed me up. I realized that I was still in love with her but I knew we would never be together because I was married to Jeri now, and God didn't like divorce.

We sat and talked for about thirty minutes before I left. While I was driving home, all I could think about was Betty Jean and how I wished things had turned out differently. I will always remember that night because that was the last time I saw Nelson, or Velma, or Betty Jean.

I was still going to church a lot and hanging out with Campbell and Kennedy. We were sitting in the pulpit one night when Bishop Campbell handed me a piece of paper. After looking at it, I realized it was an ordination certificate, officially making me an elder in the Church of God in Christ. He said that after observing me, he decided to recognize my Baptist ordination. That night I became, Elder Barr.

One of the things I really liked about the COGIC were the "Preach off's" (not the official name) that went on sometimes. That was when several preachers would preach, one behind the other, for about five minutes each. They were always fun because the Spirit was very high, and each preacher was already on fire when he stood up. At first I was nervous about preaching behind Elder Campbell, but I discovered that it worked to my advantage, because he was so full of fire, who ever came behind him was on fire too.

That was what happened one night when we were at another church. Campbell had preached everybody crazy. Then, Kennedy got up and preached like I had never heard him preach before. When he sat down, I got up, stomping as usual. I was starting to really get into the sermon when I saw Campbell trying to get my attention. The floorboard of the pulpit was loose, so every time I stomped it was shaking the P.A. system. I didn't stop preaching, I just quit stomping, and for the first time in my life, I was hooping.

I had never felt the Spirit of God come over me the way He did that night. When worship service was over, we were hugging each other and praising God for the way He had used and blessed us that night. I really love those two brothers.

That was a very special night in more ways than one. I didn't know it at the time, but it would be 25 years before I would stand in the pulpit and preach the Word of God again.

CHAPTER THREE

The Fall

I was under pressure from every angle imaginable. Satan definitely had me on his hit list. I had a new boss at Woolworth's, Mr. Moore, and he came in making my life miserable. He was uncomfortable with a preacher working for him, but he couldn't fire me. Only the corporate office could do that, so he tried to make me quit. He was always on my case.

As if that wasn't bad enough, my co-workers were constantly trying to get me to party with them after work, my mother kept telling me that I was too young to be in church so much, and although Jeri was pregnant with our second child (my first), our relationship was falling apart. In all honesty, it was not all Jeri's fault. I had my own ideas of what a marriage was supposed to be like. They were mostly based on television shows like "Leave it to Beaver," "Father knows best," and "The Dick Van Dyke Show." They never had a problem that the husband couldn't solve in 30 minutes or less.

I ended up dealing with problems the way I had seen my father deal with them. I would leave the house instead of staying and trying to work things out. Sure, Jeri had her shortcomings, but so did I. It was just easier for me to dwell on her faults than to deal with my own.

One evening, Vivian came to the house to visit Jeri. They had become good friends. While Vivian was waiting for Jeri to come out of the bedroom, she said she had something she wanted me to see. Vivian had been going through some papers and ran across an old picture. She handed it to me. It was a picture of Betty Jean. I then realized that the main problem with our relationship was that I was married to Jeri, but I had never gotten over Betty Jean or Charlotte either for that matter. Nevertheless, I loved Jeri and I wanted to make our marriage work.

Woolworth's only had one black store manager in the entire Chicago region. His name was Sammy Wayne. Sammy managed the store in downtown Gary, Indiana, on Broadway. He was, as they say, a legend in his own time. He was well-known throughout the company and had the reputation of being one of the best and brightest managers in the region. I was happy when

Sammy took me under his wing and tried to help me move up in the company.

Sammy came to my house one Saturday evening. He was going to a nightclub and was trying to talk me into going with him. My mother was there at the time and was telling me that I should go and have some fun. When I told Sammy I didn't drink, he said, "You don't have to drink liquor. You can drink water if you want. You drink water don't you?" I decided to go to the club.

When we got there, I didn't have any trouble getting in even though I was only 20 years old. We sat at a table with some people that Sammy knew. Some of them were teasing me because I wasn't drinking, so after a while I went ahead and ordered a beer. I started loosening up and getting into the party. It had been years since I had danced, but I started dancing and drinking more beer.

We left there and went to another club, and then to another club, and then to another club. By the time I got home I was so drunk, I threw up. The next day was Sunday, and for the first time in I don't know how long, I didn't go to church. I was feeling guilty because of what I had done. Because of the teachings I'd had under Nelson, I thought I was no longer saved. I couldn't be. I had been in a nightclub and I was drinking and dancing with a bunch of sinners.

Elder Campbell called me that evening to see if I was all right. I told him I wasn't feeling well. When I didn't go to church all week, he called me again. I told him I had been working late.

The next Saturday, I went to a club on the south side, The Bird Cage, with some other store managers and trainees. While we were riding, someone lit a marijuana joint and passed it to Claude. After he took a couple of hits he passed it to me. I had never smoked marijuana before, but I didn't want everyone to know that I wasn't as cool as they thought I was, so I took it. I took a couple of hits like I had seen Claude do and passed it on.

Just like the week before, we went club hopping, and just like the week before, I went home drunk, but that time I was also high. Also, just like the week before, I didn't go to church and Campbell called to see what was going on. He asked me if I was all right and said that he was concerned about me. I gave him some line about the job. When Kennedy called, I told him the same thing.

I was drifting further and further away from God and the church, and I didn't know what to do. Once again, I didn't show up to church all week, and Campbell knew something was wrong. He kept calling me, trying to get me back to church. I was glad when my phone got disconnected because Campbell couldn't call to bug me anymore. That Saturday evening, after I got home from work, the doorbell rang. It was Campbell. He knew I was in trouble and was trying to get me back in church and to the Lord.

I don't know what I said to him. I was already drunk. Jeri told me I cursed him out. All I know is, that brother loved me so much, and he was so serious about his ministry, that he did everything he could to win me back to the Lord. As long as I live I will never forget him. Elder Willie James Campbell is truly a child of God, and a good friend too. It would be a long time before I would see Dub again, but he never stopped praying for me.

I started going to a non-denominational church on 76th and Cottage Grove, but I didn't want to be in the pulpit. I only went every once in a while, and after a few weeks, I stopped going to church all together. I started drinking and smoking weed more often. I tried to justify my leaving the church. I said none of the churches were right. In other words, there was no perfect church or denomination. I told Jeri she had been right about the Church of God in Christ. I think she was glad I had left St. James. I had become a "Little Dub." I had started talking like him and acting like him. I had even shaped my mustache like his, the Fu-Man-Chew style.

The truth was, there was nothing wrong with the church. It was me. Like the lost sheep that Jesus talked about in St. Luke, I had strayed away from my Shepherd (God) and had gotten lost. I strayed away the same way sheep stray away from their Shepard - I nibbled myself away.

There might be a herd of sheep walking along, following the shepherd and the rest of the sheep, but at the same time they will be nibbling on the grass. They will nibble a little, and then they will look up to make sure they are still following the shepherd and the other sheep. However, sometimes there is that one sheep or that one lamb that gets so engrossed in his nibbling that he forgets to look up. He just wanders along with his head down. He's enjoying the grass so much that he just nibbles, and nibbles, and nibbles. And when he finally does look up, he doesn't see the shepherd or the rest of the sheep. He is lost. He has wandered off in the wrong direction and he cannot find his way back. He didn't mean to get lost. He just nibbled himself away from the fold.

Our jails, prisons, and cemeteries are full of men and women who have nibbled themselves away from God. They've nibbled themselves away from the church. They've nibbled themselves away from everything they have been taught. They're not bad people. They were just nibbling.

I started nibbling when I started hanging with some of the people I worked with. You can be friends with someone without hanging out in their playground or playing with their toys.

Woolworth's transferred me to the other store in Gary, Indiana. That was Mr. Moore's way of getting rid of me. The store was in the Tri-City Plaza Shopping Center, a 40-mile drive from my house. The manager's name was Dave. He seemed to be all right at first, but I found out that he was very prejudiced.

I was walking down Christiana one afternoon when I ran into Fuzzy. He didn't know that I had left the church, so when I walked up to him he said, "Don't start preaching to me, Bub. I don't want to hear it." I told him I wasn't preaching anymore and asked him where we could get some weed. We walked down the street to Roosevelt and Christiana to a tavern called Heat Wave. Fuzzy introduced me to Brown, who sold nickel bags in front of the tavern. We bought a bag from Brown and a quart of beer from the tavern. Then we went to my apartment to get high.

Jeri didn't mind us drinking beer in the house, but we had to smoke our weed on the back porch. That was the first time Fuzzy and I had hung out together in a long time. There was a lot to talk about and catch up on. We had been through a lot together before I was saved (became a Christian) and were glad to be friends again.

There was one person that was not happy at all with my new lifestyle, my dad. He constantly tried talking to me and letting me know that I was a preacher and God wasn't pleased with what I was doing but I wouldn't listen to him. My mind was made up. I was not a preacher anymore. I had quit.

I started hanging out with my brother, Ralph. It had been a long time since we had been together. Ralph had gotten an apartment with his girlfriend, Deborah. Sometimes I went to his place after work and we would get high and talk about old times. I was so glad to be with my little brother again.

Most of the time we would drink beer, smoke weed, and listen to jazz. I had gotten into jazz when I started getting high. I had heard that jazz musicians were high when they played their tunes, so I figured that I could enjoy it more if I was high while I was listening to it.

Dave's brother was a real estate agent in the Gary, IN. area. He had a house that he wanted to rent to Jeri and me. We drove out there to see it one night, and boy were we surprised. First of all, the house was located on a dirt road. The streets were not paved and there were no sidewalks.

The bedrooms were on the second floor but the trick was getting up there. There was a rope that hung from the ceiling in the kitchen. When you pulled the rope, something that looked like a fire escape came down. The steps were metal. Although it was a nice looking house and close to my job, there was no way I was going to move my family there. That "stairway" was dangerous for my pregnant wife and my three-year-old son.

Dave was angry when I told him we were not going to take to the house. He said I was stupid for turning it down and continuing to live in Chicago. Then he told me that it was my decision, but I had better not be late, or not make it to work because of the long drive. I took offence to what he said and the way he said it. At first I didn't say anything, but I started thinking about all of the racist statements that he had been making. I was very angry, so, I confronted Dave and told him what I thought of him. After that, we didn't have a lot to do with each other, which was fine with me.

One night I came home very drunk. Jeri was already angry about something, and my coming in that late and that drunk, didn't help matters. I went to bed but Jeri wouldn't let me go to sleep. She wanted to argue. Then, I did something that I swore I never would do. I beat up my wife just like my father beat up my mother so many times before. The difference was, Jeri was about seven or eight months pregnant.

I was drunk, but I wasn't stupid. I wasn't about to go to sleep in that house after hitting Jeri. I got dressed and went to Fuzzy's house. I went home the next day and apologized. Although we had a lot of problems in our marriage, we had a lot of good times too. I really did love Jeri but I didn't know how to show it. My lack of problem solving skills also didn't help matters any.

On Sunday, July 13th, Fuzzy and I were at my house drinking and getting high when Jeri told me that it was time for her to go to the hospital. Fuzzy rode with us, and I took Jeri to Mt. Sinai Hospital. After they took her to the delivery room, Fuzzy and I went to the waiting room. After about 20 or 30 minutes, we decided to leave and get something else to drink. We were planning on going back to the hospital but we never made it. We were too drunk. By the time I sobered up, I found out that Jeri had a baby girl and had named her Andrea Patrice Barr. She was a beautiful little thing and I was as proud as I could be. I vowed to be a better husband and a good father to Everett and Andrea, who we called Andi.

When I got to work one day, Dave called me in the office. He told me that there was money missing from the cash drawer in the office and he accused me of taking it. He said he didn't want me in the office or on the sales floor anymore. He said that as far as he was concerned, from that time on, I was just an over-paid stock boy.

I wasn't about to take that. I cursed him out and left the store. I had never taken anything from that store. I didn't know whether someone else had gotten into the office or he took the money himself and was trying to blame me. Besides, the office wasn't enclosed. Anybody could have climbed over that wall, but I didn't care. I was tired of his racist remarks. Since I wasn't saved or in church anymore, I didn't have a problem with kicking off in his behind, and I told him that.

I drove to the corporate office in Desplains and told the district manager what had happened. He gave me an immediate transfer to one of the stores in downtown Chicago, on State Street and Jackson. It was a huge store. The manager, Mr. Howell, looked, and dressed like the late mob boss, John Gotti, the Dapper Don.

I didn't have any responsibilities there. I wasn't really a part of the management team. All I did everyday was stock shelves and build displays. I was starting to hate that store, that job, and that company. Whenever I could think of a good excuse, I didn't go to work.

On Saturday morning, August 24th, I woke up with a huge hangover. I really didn't want to go to work that day, but I couldn't come up with an excuse that I hadn't already used. I was so hung over I couldn't think. My brain was hurting.

While I was driving to the El station (the subway), I was still trying to think of a reason not to go in. I always parked at the El station closest to my house and rode the train because parking downtown was too expensive. I tried to park in a very tight spot, and while I was backing in, I tapped the car that was parked behind me. I had my excuse. I found a pay phone and called the store. I told them I wouldn't be in because I had been in an accident.

When I got back to Christiana, I saw Cy sitting on his front porch. He was drinking some whiskey and beer. I started drinking with him. When that was gone, we went to the liquor store and bought more. Sitting on that porch and drinking on an empty stomach in the hot sun that early in the morning was not very smart. I felt really sick. I staggered down the street to my house and passed out.

Some time later, the doorbell wakened me. It was, Ralph, his girlfriend, Deborah, and my mother. They had just come from city hall where Ralph and Debbie had gotten married. They wanted to celebrate, but I was in no shape. Besides, there was a lot of tension between Jeri and me. I was sitting at the bar and Jeri was standing in the middle of the floor. We were staring at each other real hard.

All of a sudden, Ralph started instigating. He said, "What is this, a staring contest?" I said, "Yeah." Then he said, "Who is the baddest?" I said, "I'm the baddest." Then I staggered over to Jeri and hit her in her jaw. When Ralph saw what was happening, he grabbed me so I couldn't hit her again. While he was holding me, I felt something wet and sticky rolling down my face and dripping onto my arm. I thought I was sweating, but when I looked at it, I realized it was blood, my blood. Jeri had hit me in my forehead with a high heeled shoe.

I went crazy. Jeri ran out of the door and down the stairs, and I was right behind her. She ran to my parent's house next door trying to get away from me, but I caught up with her in the living room. I threw her onto one of the chairs and started choking her. I was completely out of control. Mother, dad, Ralph, and Deborah were all trying to pull me off of her, but they couldn't get my hands from around her neck. I was trying to kill her. Finally, my father pulled me off of her and she ran into my mother's bedroom, locked the door, and called the police. I broke away from my father and tried to kick the door down.

Ralph and my father dragged me out into the hallway. That was where I was when the police came. They talked to Jeri first, and then they came out and talked to me. They could see that I was drunk. After talking to my father, they decided not to take me to jail. When they left, dad told me to go home and go to sleep. I did what he said.

There were times in my life that I went to jail when I really shouldn't have gone. However, that was one of the times that I didn't go to jail when I really should have. Drunkenness is no excuse for hitting a woman. There are no excuses.

When I woke up, I went outside just in time to see Jeri getting into a car. Her sister, Lois, had driven from Detroit to pick her up. I was still drunk and my head was starting to hurt, but I started drinking and partying again anyway. I hung out with my cousin, Rose, and her husband, Troy, the rest of the night. That was the first time I had met him, and he teased me all night long about the knot on my head. When I got home it dawned on me that after 53 weeks of marriage, I was alone again.

I started spending more time at Ralph and Deborah's house. Ralph and I would smoke weed, drink whiskey and beer and listen to jazz. He also became my barber. One day I picked up some beer and went to his house so he could cut my hair. When he came to the door, he had a strange look on his face. After I went in and sat down, he showed me a letter that he had received. It was a draft notice. My baby brother was going into the Army.

Jeri and I had an on again, off again relationship for the next two years. During that time, Gip had gotten out of the Marines. He and Vivian had gotten married and had an apartment on Homan and Grenshaw. Jeri and I hung out with them a lot. Almost every night we were at their apartment or they were at ours. I was glad that Gip had come back from Nam in one piece, but Butch and Don, Cy's little brother, were still there. I was very worried about Ralph having to go.

I finally turned 21 in October of that year. Until then, I had been using Fuzzy's I.D. card to get into nightclubs and buy liquor. One of the clubs I went to was at Roosevelt and Albany (I don't remember the name of it). One Saturday night, Chucky came to my crib. He had some pills that he called trees (short for Christmas trees). I took two of them, and then we walked down Roosevelt to the club. He told me to watch myself because those trees would sneak up on me. Boy was he right. About an hour or so later, everything was just a big blur. I tried to find Chucky so we could get out of there, but I kept bumping into people. Finally I decided to get out of there and go home.

It was about a five block walk down Roosevelt from Albany to Christiana, and for five blocks I was leaning on one building after another. I don't know how I managed to get across any of those streets, but I had never been so glad to almost see my house. When I was about three houses away from my door, I saw a gang of men coming towards me. It looked like it was a couple hundred of them, but I found out later that there were only four.

When they saw the condition I was in, they robbed me, taking my wallet and my watch. I was so high, I couldn't fight, I couldn't run, and I couldn't yell. All I could do was just lie there against that building while they were hitting me and going through my pockets, hoping they would hurry up and finish robbing me so I could go in the house and lie down.

The next day I found out that Chucky and Gip had been looking for me at the club. They said that one minute they saw me, the next minute they didn't. After that incident, I knew that I didn't want to mess with any more trees.

THE HOODLUM PREACHER

I decided to leave Woolworth's. It had become apparent that I was never going to be a manager, and Sammy confirmed my suspicions. He told me that I was at a dead end store because of the problems I'd had in the store in Gary, Indiana. I was labeled a thief and a troublemaker. At that time, I had never stolen anything in my life (except a Playboy book when I was about ten years old). So I quit.

I was out of work for several months before I started working with Nehemiah. He was the captain of the 17th precinct in the 24th Ward. I was his assistant. The alderman and ward committeeman was George W. Collins. He sent me to the city of Chicago's Department of Weights and Measures where I started working in the Model Cities Program as a deputy inspector. That was the way Chicago politics worked back then. It was called the patronage system. In order to work in city, county, or state government, you had to be sponsored by a ward committeeman and work in one of the precincts. But in reality, we all worked for Mayor Richard J. Daily. Later that year, Alderman Collins was elected to the U. S. Congress, and became one of the two first black congressmen from Chicago.

I was so happy to be working again; I just wanted to celebrate when I got home. When I saw my father, he told me that the police were looking for me. He said that Jeri had called them on me and told them that I was armed and dangerous. All I could think about was losing the job that I had just gotten after being unemployed for so long, or the police killing me for nothing. I was furious.

I bought a fifth of liquor, put a chair in the middle of the living room floor, turned off all of the lights, and sat there drinking and waiting for Jeri to come home so I could kill her before the police killed me. She never came home, so I killed the house instead. I pulled the carpeting off of the floor, took the pictures off of the walls and broke them, threw the cocktail table off of the back porch, and tore up everything in sight. When I woke up the next day, it looked like the Vietnam War had been fought in my apartment. Needless to say, Jeri and I broke up again.

My apartment became the party capital of the neighborhood. Some nights there were more people at my place

60

than there were at the neighborhood bars. On weekends, after the lounges closed, everybody went to my house, and we partied the rest of the night away.

My life was getting more and more out of control, but I couldn't see it at the time. It was kind of like the day Chucky and I walked to Miss Jenkins' store. I was about 13 years old at the time. Chucky had a dog, named Champ, and he took him to the store with us. Since Champ couldn't go into the store, Chucky handed me the leash so I could hold him until he came out. But when Chucky disappeared into the store, Champ turned on me and started chasing me down the street. As I was running, people were laughing and yelling at me, but I was running so fast, I couldn't hear what they were saying. Finally, I heard one of them say, "Let go of the leash. Let go of the leash." It hadn't dawned on me that while I was trying to get away from Champ, I was still holding on to his leash. When I dropped the leash, Champ stopped chasing me and ran back to the store where Chucky was.

Sometimes you can get rid of some of your problems if you just let go of the leash. There might be some friends that don't mean you any good. You need to let go of the leash. Leave them alone. You might be in a relationship that is coming between you and God. You need to let go of the leash. Let them go. You might have started doing some things that you are not comfortable with, so you can fit in with the crowd, and now your life is becoming unmanageable. You need to listen to the voice of God. He might be telling you to let go of the leash.

Herbie Mann had just come out with a new album, "Memphis Underground." I became a Herbie Mann fan. I bought all of his records I could find, but my favorites were (and still are) "Summertime" and "Coming Home Baby."

Before I left Woolworth's, I started hanging out with Tadpole a lot. He had been one of Ralph's friends. Tadpole was Cy and Don's cousin. He kind of took Ralph's place while he was away. We just drank, smoked weed, and listened to jazz; we also started snorting (sniffing) duji.

Duji was an inexpensive high (so I thought). It came in small, clear capsules, so it was also called buttons. A button only cost three dollars, and it was enough for two people to get high and

61

nod. We had become best friends, so we would get together every Friday or Saturday and snort duji, listen to some jazz, and just nod off.

One Friday evening, I was at home waiting for Tadpole. It was his turn to buy the buttons. When he got there, B.B. and Ronnie were with him. We had all grown up together, and B.B. had been with Nelson during the same time I was. He had also been in the choir with me at Rev. Jones' church. Now we had both left the church.

We all went into the dining room and I pulled out an album cover for them to put the duji on. But instead, they were taking needles and eyedroppers from a paper bag. Tadpole started cooking the duji in a top. Then he said we were going to shoot the stuff this time instead of snorting it. I told them to go ahead and shoot theirs. Just put mine on the album cover. Then he said, "Bub, you don't understand, we're shooting ours, and you're shooting yours too."

I hadn't noticed B.B. and Ronnie standing behind me until it was too late. They grabbed me from behind and held me while Tadpole wrapped one of my neckties around my arm, just above the elbow. Then he said, "Sorry Bub, but I know that this is the only way we can get you to try it." As he was sticking the needle into my arm, I was still struggling. Then he said, "You better quit struggling before the needle breaks off in your arm." I stopped struggling, but I had made up my mind that when they let me go, I was going to get my gun and blow all three of them away.

When the drugs started going through my system, I felt better than I had ever felt before. It felt better than sex. It was an instant high. I wanted to shoot up all of the time. After that night we never snorted the duji anymore. We always shot it. The problem was, I couldn't hit myself (find my vein and shoot the dope in it). We ended up going from buying one or two buttons every weekend, to buying one or two buttons everyday.

Since I couldn't hit myself, I always had to get to someone hit me. Therefore, I had to share my drugs with them. It had been the same as when I started buying reefer. I didn't know how to roll a joint, so I was never able to get high by myself and I always had to share my stuff with someone else. Just like I had decided it was time to learn how to roll reefer, I decided it was time for me to learn how to hit myself. I must say it was a very painful lesson.

There were a few people that I used to shoot up with. One of them was Willie. He was part of the crowd that was older than us when we were growing up. One Saturday, Willie came to my house. When I went to the door he said, "Come on Bub. Let's go shoot some dope."

Maybe it was the way he said it, "Let's go shoot some dope." I didn't mess with dope. Dope was hard drugs. All I did was smoke a little reefer, pop a few pills, and shoot a little duji, but here he was, talking about shooting some dope.

I asked him what kind of dope he was talking about shooting. He said, "We're gonna shoot some heroin." My father had always told me to stay away from heroin. I always justified using the drugs that I was using because I was able to say, "At least it's not heroin." So I told Willie that I didn't shoot heroin. When I said that, he gave me a weird look. He said, "You don't shoot heroin?" I said, "No." He said, "Well, what do you shoot?" I said, "I don't shoot nothing but duji." Then he said, "What do you think duji is, fool?"

I couldn't believe it. I had been shooting heroin all that time and didn't know it. When I saw Tadpole I asked him if he knew that we had been shooting heroin. He said, "Yeah. Didn't you?" I felt like a complete idiot, but it was too late. I liked it too much.

Don't get me wrong. I'm not blaming anyone for the decisions I made. I decided to leave the church. I decided to drink liquor. I decided to smoke reefer. I decided to snort duji. Although I didn't know it was heroin, I knew it was wrong. So what if I was forced or tricked into shooting up that first time? I shouldn't have been messing with it in the first place. I put myself in that position. It was my own fault. It was like the time I was driving down Davison and enjoying the ride, when suddenly I found myself on the Davison freeway. Only now I was on a different freeway, "The Drug Freeway." Just like the Davison, I didn't know how to get off.

Tadpole and I started hanging out with Steve, another junkie in the neighborhood. Steve was a former college basketball star who was living in the basement of his mother's house on Spaulding Avenue. The basement also served as a shooting gallery. A shooting gallery is a place where junkies would pay whoever lived there $2.00 or give them some of their dope so they could take off (shoot up) there. Sometimes the people who ran the galleries had extra "fits" for sale, rental, or use. The equipment needed to shoot drugs is called fits, short for outfits, or "works." They consisted of needles, syringes or droppers, cookers, and ties.

Droppers were eyedroppers that were taken from Murine Eye Drops boxes. We would put a needle on the end of the dropper and use it to shoot the drugs. In those days most of us used droppers instead of syringes. The Murine Company eventually had to change the packaging of their products because all of the eyedroppers were being stolen from the store selves. Cookers are what the drugs are cooked or dissolved in. It could be a tablespoon or a Richard's Wild Irish Rose wine top. A tie is a belt, a shoestring, a necktie or whatever you can use to tie up your arm to make your veins stand out.

Sometimes, Steve's place would be full of men and women who were taking off. Some of them could no longer get a hit in the veins in their arms, so they were shooting in their hands, feet or even between their legs. Some of them had people shooting the dope in the veins in their necks because that was the only place they could get a hit. I was shooting up with Steve and some of his friends more and more. Sometimes, I would go to his place; sometimes, they would go to mine.

One day, Tadpole came to my apartment with a strange look on his face. I had seen that look before. It was the same look that Ralph had when he had been drafted. When Tadpole handed me an envelope, I already knew what it said. He, too, had been drafted.

The city put up trailers in each of the four targeted neighborhoods of the "Model Cities Program." Two of them were on the south side, one on the north side, and one on the west side. That was where I worked. The area is called Lawndale. My boss was a very beautiful lady named Joyce. She was about 20 years my senior and had been in the political game for a long time. She knew what she was doing. We became very close and hung out together a lot during work hours and afterwards. Eventually, we became more than just co-workers.

The north side office was all white. The other offices were all black. The black employees were being discriminated against, so we went to city hall to talk to the commissioner, Jane Byrne. Since I was a former minister and had experience in public speaking, I was chosen to be the spokesperson.

The meeting didn't go well at all. I could tell from the beginning that Commissioner Byrne had no respect for us. Shortly after the meeting, I was reassigned. I was no longer inspecting stores. I was inspecting gas pumps, in the middle of January, in Chicago.

To inspect a gas pump, you pump five gallons of gas into a can. Then you make sure that both the can and the pump register at five gallons. You, then, would carry the gas to the storage tank and pour it in. Then you pump another five gallons, make sure that the can registers at five gallons and the pump registers at ten. Then you have to check the price to make sure it is right. Then you poured that gas into the storage tank. Then you go to the next tank and start all over. There were some stations that had as many as twenty pumps. I almost froze to death.

I guess that was Ms. Byrne's way of sending a message to the rest of the blacks. "Don't mess with me." So I sent a message back to her. I can't tell you what it was because I don't use that kind of language anymore, but I can tell you that after three days on the gas pumps, I quit.

I found out later that if I would have told Congressman Collins, who was my sponsor, what was going on, he could have stepped in on my behalf. My father had been noticing some of the unscrupulous things that I was doing: stealing votes, bribing voters, and taking bribes myself. He was always trying to tell me that what I was doing was wrong. He said, "You're a preacher, man. You can't live just any kind of way." The problem was, I wasn't a preacher anymore. I had quit. After that experience, I decided I didn't want to be a politician anymore either. So I said, "To hell with politics." I was unemployed again.

I got a job working as a security guard on the midnight shift. One night I decided not to go to work. I was sitting home when the doorbell rang. I started to answer it but changed my mind. When it kept ringing, I thought that someone was trying to make sure I wasn't home. I was right. A few minutes later, I heard someone on the back porch messing with the windows. My apartment had been broken into several times. I figured these were the same dudes coming back again.

I got my gun and crouched down behind the wall. I heard the glass break and the window being opened. I peeked around the corner and watched them as they stepped through the open window. When they were inside, I stood up and turned on the lights. You should have seen their faces when they looked up and saw me standing there with a gun in my hand. I was just as shocked as they were when I saw who it was.

It was Frank, Steve's brother, who was also one of my "getting high" buddies, with one of his friends. I was so mad, I started to shoot both of them. Instead, I called the police. The next day, I found out that the police took them outside and let them go. I also found out that they were the ones that had broken into my house before. So, I went looking for them. When I knocked on Steve's door, I had the gun in my hand. It almost scared his mother to death. Steve told me that Frank had moved. He said that he heard what Frank had done and that he was sorry. I didn't want to hear that. I started to shoot him just for being Frank's brother. I wanted to shoot his mother too for giving birth to him.

The night shift wasn't working for me. I worked from 11:00pm to 7:00am, but I didn't have sense enough to go to bed when I got off. After three nights, I changed jobs and went to a small, black-owned security company that was across the street from my former job, the Model Cities office. I think I liked being a security guard because I could carry a gun.

I was there for a week and had never caught anyone stealing. I was starting to wonder if I was in the wrong line of work. Some of my co-workers were wondering the same thing. I was working in plain clothes at a grocery store one day when I saw a man stuffing a small ham under his shirt. He was a pretty big brother, but I didn't care. I took him to the backroom, but before I could search him, he stuck his hand in one of his pockets. I didn't know what he was reaching for, so I hit his hand with my blackjack. Turns out, he was reaching for money to bribe me, but I didn't want it. I finally caught someone and I needed that arrest to keep my job. I called the police and rode with them to the main lock-up at 11th and State Street. I felt like I was one of them.

When I left the store that evening I was feeling good. I couldn't wait to get to the office with my very first arrest report. I was waiting for a bus, when I heard a horn blowing. When I looked around, I saw that it was Red, one of Ralph's friends that lived on the next block from me. He asked me if I wanted a ride. I got into the car, but before we went one block, we were pulled over by the "Slick Boys," (The Chicago Police Department's Narcotic Detectives). I wasn't worried, though, I was one of them. I was a security guard.

Red walked back to their car to see what they wanted. While I was sitting in the car, one of them came to the window. He said, "Your partner's got a lot of stuff in his pocket. Do you have any?" I showed him my badge and told him I was a security guard and had a gun in my holster. He stepped back, pointed his gun at my head and told me to put my hands on the dashboard. He handcuffed me and put me in their car. I asked him if I could get my arrest report out of the car. He said, "You won't need it. You've got your own arrest report now." I guess I wasn't one of them after all.

I was charged with unlawful use of a weapon, my very first felony. Red had some weed in his pocket, so he was charged with that. We were taken to the Filmore district station and placed in a holding cell. Ironically, that was the station I used to want to work at when I was a child, and wanted to be a policeman. My bond was $1000.00, meaning I needed $100.00 to get out. I found out that if I didn't make bail, I would be taken to 11th and State, the same lock-up they had taken the brother that I hit with my blackjack.

All I could think about was ending up in a cell with him (without my blackjack), or in a lock-up at the Cook County Jail and him telling everyone how he got there. So I called dad and he came and got me. Red called his father, and his father bailed him out too.

Oh! I forgot to mention something. Red's father was also a preacher. When I went to work the next day, I was told that I couldn't return until the court case was over. I was out of work again.

I was sitting home one day when the doorbell rang. It was Tadpole. He had been kicked out of the Army with an undesirable discharge because of his drug habit. Boy, was I glad to see him. We picked up where we had left off, shooting dope.

At one point, we owed all of the drug dealers in the area, so we were dodging them. One day, we were going to cop some "boy" (heroin). I started walking north, towards Roosevelt, but Tadpole said he couldn't go that way because he owed Johnny. So he started walking south, towards 13th street, but I told him that I couldn't go that way because I owed Poopy. So I started walking east, toward Spaulding, but he said we couldn't go that way because he owed Peanut. So he started walking west, towards Homan, but I told him that I couldn't go that way because I owed Coleman. We decided to split up and meet up on Roosevelt and Kedzie.

One of my childhood friends, nicknamed Huckabuck, was shot and killed by someone he was fighting. Huckabuck was a short, muscle-bound brother who wasn't afraid of anyone or anything. His mother and sisters had just moved into the building across the street from me. His younger brother, Michael, was in the Marine Corp.

Shortly after that, two other friends of mine, Lucas and Richard Curtis, were shot down in "The Enchanted," a neighborhood nightclub. They were leaders of the defunct street gang, the Roman Saints, and had run off with some grant money that the gang had received. Lucas died but Richard survived and later joined the Army.

Michael got a hardship discharge from the Marines, and we became good friends. He was just like his brother, Huckabuck. He was short, muscle-bound, and crazy. He looked like, and was built like Mike Tyson. Mike was always trying to get me to stop shooting dope. He talked about how bad my arms were starting to look. We stayed high all of the time, drinking fifths of gin and dropping Red Devils (pills).

Mike was dating a married lady that lived in his building. Her husband worked nights. When he went to work, so did Mike. One night, after she took her husband to work, she let us use their car. When we were walking to the car, a man walked past us. Mike didn't say anything, he just hit him in his jaw knocking him out cold. Then he reached into the man's pockets and took his money. We got in the car and drove off. We went to a club somewhere, but we were so high, we couldn't remember where we had parked the car and ended up taking a cab home. The next morning, Mike came to my house and said that his girlfriend was freaking out because her husband was about to get off work and the car wasn't there. We borrowed someone else's car and drove around until we found it.

A lot of people were afraid of Mike. They said he was a big bully just like his older brother, Huckabuck. People couldn't understand why I hung out with him. They said he was crazy and had a death wish, but Michael was my friend. In a sense, I think I replaced his brother.

When I went to court for the gun charge, the judge told me that he would dismiss the charges if my employers came to court and verified the fact that I worked for them and that it was their gun. He gave me a 30 day continuance. I went to the office and told them what the judge had said. They assured me that they would be there on my next court date. They didn't show. I was given another continuance.

Tadpole and I continued to get high. One night we didn't have any money, so I decided to walk to Sears and write a check from an account I had with their bank. The problem was I didn't have any money in the account. Since the bank was closed at the time, I figured what they didn't know, wouldn't hurt me. I gave the cashier the check and was waiting for her to come back to the window with my money. The police came instead. At that time, Sears had their own police force that was composed of off-duty city policemen. It turned out that one of my checks had bounced a week or so before.

The officer took me to the security office. I gave him some sob story about needing the money because of my mother and told him I had always re-paid any bad checks I had written. I was even able to muster up a few tears while I was talking to him. To my surprise, he not only let me go, but he took me back upstairs to the cashier and told her to go ahead and cash my check. That was when I started thinking that I could talk my way out of anything. When I left Sears, I copped two bags of blow (heroin), and Tadpole and I got high.

Jeri called me one day and offered to send me a bus ticket to Detroit if I wanted to go. I said okay. Her father picked me up at the Greyhound station. Jeri was renting a nice little house on Manor. We'd had another daughter, Vivian, who was named after Gip's wife. She was about a year old. We were living as a family again. I enjoyed playing with Everett and Andi (Andrea) who were five and three years old at the time. I also enjoyed doing things around the house.

I started hanging out with Marvin, Jeri's friend's husband. At first we just rode around, drinking beer and smoking weed. Before long, we were shooting heroin. Whenever I smoked weed at home, I went outside in the back yard, or in the basement. It was during one of those trips to the basement that I found a book about the life of Huey P. Newton, founder of the Black Panther Party. That book would later play a major part in my life.

I had to return to Chicago to stand trial on the gun charge. Before I left, I spent a little time with Everett and Andi, and then I took Vivian out of her crib and played with her for a while. I bought a round trip ticket and boarded a Greyhound bus late that night. My plan was to go to court the next morning, and return to Detroit that evening. I got to Chicago at about 6:00 or 7:00 that morning. When I got to my parent's house, I had a message to call Jeri. When I called her, I got the bad news. Vivian, our youngest daughter, was dead. She had gotten sick that night and Jeri took her to the hospital. She died in the waiting room.

When I got to court, I was messed up in the head. What made it worse, my employers didn't show up again. The Judge wanted to give me another continuance, but I didn't want it. I just wanted to plead guilty and get it over with. The judge tried to talk me out of pleading guilty, but I wasn't hearing it. It was clear to me that my employers were never going to show up, and I was just tired of it. The judge accepted my plea and sentenced me to one-year probation. I was glad that it was over with, but now I had a felony record. I didn't realize how much it would affect my life.

I went to the security guard office and demanded my last paycheck. They said I couldn't get it until I returned their gun. They could have had their gun months ago if they had gone to court with me, and they knew it. I planned to get even. That night I got a gas can and filled it up. I was going to burn their building down. I'm glad Michael talked me out of it. The only thing I had ever burned was a pot of oatmeal. Besides, I had to get back to Detroit. I had a daughter to bury.

We had a family hour for Vivian at one of the local funeral homes. She looked so beautiful lying there. My father and a few others came in from Chicago, but mostly it was Jeri's family and friends.

I was drinking and drugging more and more. Marvin and I were shooting up everyday. One night, I needed drugs so bad, I stole Jeri's money by staging a break in while she was asleep. Afterwards, I felt like a low down dirty dog. This woman was scrimping and scraping to feed our children, and here I was, stealing the money to buy heroin. She never said anything, but I believe that she knew that I was the one who stole the money.

I decided it would be better if I left. Like the saying goes, she could do bad all by herself. So one day while Jeri was away, I told Everett I was going to the store. Instead, I went to the Greyhound bus station and bought a one-way ticket to Chicago. However, things were different. I was no longer an average citizen. Now, I was a convicted felon.

THE HOODLUM PREACHER

CHAPTER FOUR

The Marine

Ralph was out of the Army and living on the first floor of our family building on Christiana with Deborah and their daughter, Valisha, who was born while they were in Germany. I hung out with him sometimes, drinking beer, smoking weed, and listening to jazz. However, most of the time, I shot heroin with Tadpole or dropped reds with Mike.

One day, I caught the bus to the projects on Madison and Western to get more reds. I had just gotten off of the bus and was walking towards the building when I heard someone calling my name. When I turned around I saw the same two detectives that had locked me up on the gun charge. They called me over to the car, patted me down, and asked what I was doing in that neighborhood. I told them I was catching the bus and going home. They reminded me that I was on probation and let me know that they were watching me.

It seemed like I was getting stopped practically every day for something, and I had only been on probation a month. I still had eleven months to go. At this rate, I wasn't going to make it. I decided that the only way to keep from going to jail was to go into the Army. So I went to the recruiting station on Madison and enlisted. I had to go to court so the judge could take me off of probation. He suspended my probation pending my induction in the Army. I was scheduled to ship out on December 1, 1971.

Because of my reputation, no one believed I was going to the Army; no one, not even the police. Even when I showed them the enlistment papers, they still didn't believe it. Ralph gave me a going away party the night before I was supposed to leave, but no one showed up except Joe. He didn't believe I was going either but came by to get high with us anyway.

My Uncle Ray took me to the induction center the next morning at five. Dad and Auntee rode with us. I was still drunk from the night before. When I got out of the car, Auntee gave me a $50 dollar bill and we all waved good-bye. When they pulled off, I looked at that $50.00 and thought about getting high one more time before I left. Instead I went in and reported to the Army.

The sergeant that pulled my file told me that I couldn't join without a high school diploma or GED. I told him that the recruiter had known that I didn't have either. I showed him my enlistment papers. He said that the recruiter had made a mistake, and that the Army could not take me.

I was in a state of shock. I couldn't go back home. No one believed I was going in the first place. As I walked around trying to figure out what to do, I saw the Marine Corp recruiting office. I went in and told the sergeant my dilemma. He said the Marines would take me. I really didn't want to be a Marine, because I had seen the movie, "The D.I." starring Jack Webb. It is a movie about Marine boot camp. Faced with the choice of going to the Marines or going back home, I chose the Marines.

I asked when I could ship out. He said, "Today. How many years do you want?" I said, "Two." He said, "Why take two when you can have four?" I said, "OK. Give me four." (I told you I was still drunk from the night before.) I signed up for a four-year stretch in the United States Marine Corp.

Since I had signed up for four years, I had a choice of what M.O.S. (Military Occupation Something) category I wanted. I chose the one that consisted of correctional specialist, supply, or cook. I passed all of the exams and was put on a plane to San Diego, California. It was nighttime when we got there. We were put on a waiting bus and taken to the MCRD (Marine Corp Recruit Depot).

The bus driver told us that we'd better smoke all of the cigarettes we wanted to smoke right then, because it was going to be a long time before we smoked again. When we arrived at MCRD, all hell broke loose. The driver opened the door and a bunch of crazy men in uniforms ran on the bus hollering and screaming. We ran off of the bus and stood on some footprints that were painted on the ground, then we went to the barbershop where we were scalped.

We had to send our civilian clothes and all other personal belongings home, including my $50.00. After we were processed, we were marched to the barracks and told to go to bed. I remember lying in my bunk that night wondering what I had gotten myself into.

CHAPTER 4 - The Marine

During the first week, we were put in the hands of "Troop Handlers." They were in charge of us until the D.I.s (Drill Instructors) took over. I was given the position, "King Rat." King Rat was in charge of cleaning the duty hut and making the D. I. s or troop handlers' beds. I was given two assistants, called, House Mice. That sounds like the name of a rock band - *King Rat And The House Mice.*

We were told that boot camp would last twelve weeks but everyone had to take a physical fitness test first to make sure we were fit enough to go through the training. Whoever failed the test would have to go through four weeks of special training before starting boot camp. Nobody wanted to do that.

The test was simple, three pull-ups, twenty sit-ups, and a hundred yard dash. We were put in groups of three for the pull-ups and sit-ups, and we kept score for each other. While I was keeping score, one of the guys was only able to do two pull-ups. He and his friend tried to talk me into padding his score by saying he had done three. I said, "No. He only did two pull-ups. Since he couldn't do three, he failed."

Then it was my turn. They were keeping score for me. As hard as I tried, all I could do was one pull-up. Boy, was I embarrassed. I walked over to them and said, "OK. We can work something out. We all did three." I wasn't worried about the hundred-yard dash. I had always been a pretty fast runner. We ran in groups of ten. In my group, I came in dead last. As a matter of fact, everyone else had crossed the finish line before I had gotten to the halfway point. I didn't realize how out off shape I was. I also didn't realize most of the recruits in my platoon were 18-years old and had spent the last four years in high school. I was 23-years old and had spent the last four years smoking weed, shooting heroin, and getting drunk.

The first month of boot camp was torture. The D.I. s used that time to break you down, mentally, physically, and emotionally. They do that so that they can change the way you think, the way you act, and the way you react. In other words, they break you down so that they can rebuild you. Their goal is to make you a Marine.

I believe God does the same thing when we enlist into His Army. He sends us to "boot camp," so to speak. He changes the way we think, the way we act, and the way we react. His goal is to make us Christians. The Apostle Paul said, "If any man be in Christ, he is a new creature, old things are passed away, behold, all things are become new." *2 Cor 5:17*

I was in Platoon 3132, and we did everything as a group, including eating, sleeping, going to the toilet (head), and smoking cigarettes. One morning, one of the white recruits passed out. We found out that he was from a small town where there were no black people. Therefore, he had never seen a black person except on TV or in the movies. He was afraid to go to sleep because there was a black man in his barracks. After two nights of boot camp training and no sleep, he passed out.

I was promoted from King Rat to the platoon leader, called, "the guide." But when I couldn't climb the rope I was demoted to 1st Squad Leader. The platoon commander was Staff Sergeant Blum. The D.I.s were Sergeants Wagener and Mathern. As long as I live, I will never forget them. Their favorite place was called, "The Beach." It was a sand pit where we spent hours and hours doing push-ups, sit-ups, jumping jacks, squat thrusts, bends and thrusts, and any other torturous exercises they could think of.

The second month was geared toward combat readiness. We went to Camp Pendleton where we spent two weeks at the rifle range. The first week was spent "snapping in." Snapping in is the practice of shooting your weapon. You assume the various shooting positions, kneeling, sitting, and prone (laying down) and practice aiming and squeezing the trigger.

The second week was when we actually fired our weapons at the targets. It is called, "qualifying." The first day, I was on fire. I couldn't miss. The D.I.s and the shooting instructor were bragging about me to everybody. They were saying that on the official scoring day, I would shoot a perfect score. I didn't know why I was shooting so well, I had never fired a rifle before. Whatever the reason, I enjoyed the celebrity status.

On the second day, I didn't shoot as well. On the third day, I shot even worse. The shooting instructor accused me of cheating on Monday to get such a high score. Everyone else was getting better as the week went on, but I was getting worse. On Monday, I qualified as an Expert. On Tuesday, I was a Sharpshooter. On Wednesday, I dropped to Marksman. Thursday was the worst day; I didn't qualify at all. I knew that in order to qualify and get a medal, I was going to have to really concentrate and shoot well on Friday. I didn't. I shot worse. I was first squad leader and went "UNQ" (unqualified). None of the other guys bothered, or teased me about it though. It was good that they didn't. Maybe I couldn't shoot, but I could still kick off in their behinds.

We spent the second week at Camp Pendleton in the field learning water survival skills, how to jump out of helicopters and how to throw hand grenades. I thank God I wasn't as bad at throwing hand grenades as I was at shooting rifles. I would have wiped out my entire platoon.

When our combat training was over, we boarded the bus and headed back to MCRD. We spent the last month of boot camp perfecting our marching and drilling skills.

One evening, S/Sgt Blum and I were having a man-to-man conversation. He asked me what I thought of boot camp. I told him that I had thought it was going to be tougher than it had been. As soon as the words came out of my mouth, I knew I was going to regret saying them. About a week later, I did. We were all lined up in formation one day when S/Sgt. Blum said, "Private Barr doesn't think boot camp is tough enough. Well, we don't want to disappoint Private Barr, do we ladies?" Everyone shouted, "No sir." Then he marched us down to the pit and exercised us almost to death. I think I lost a few friends that day.

Just before graduation there was a drill competition between the platoons in our company. We had really learned a lot about marching. The most important thing that we learned was to listen carefully to the drill instructor when he was calling cadence for us. He is also telling us when to turn to the left, turn to the right, when to go forward, or when to stop. If we don't listen to him, we can really mess up.

I have found out that the Holy Spirit calls cadence for Christians as well. He tells us when to step with our left foot or when to step with our right. He tells us when to turn to the left and when to turn right. He also tells us when to go forward and when to stop. If we do not listen to Him, we can really mess up.

We won the drill competition. It was one of the happiest days in my life. Not only had I survived boot camp, but I was a leader of a winning team.

March 1, 1972 was the day we had all been waiting for, Graduation day. The men who qualified at the rifle range received their medals: expert, sharpshooter, or marksman. One person was chosen to receive a meritorious promotion to PFC (private first class). Since I went UNQ at the rifle range, I didn't receive either, but I didn't care. I had survived boot camp, and now I was a United States Marine. I was given ten days leave, after which I was to report to Fort Gordon, Georgia for training as a correctional specialist.

When I got home, everybody was glad to see me. Dad made his legendary sweet potato pie and we all had a great time. Gip and Don came by and we all went downstairs to Ralph's and listened to some jazz, smoked weed, drank liquor and talked about the military.

The next day I saw Tadpole. He asked me to buy some boy (heroin). I told him that I didn't mess with that anymore. He kept trying to talk me into it, but I said no. I was a proud Marine. For the first time in a long time I felt good about myself.

We decided to walk down to The Heatwave and get something to drink. While we were walking down Christiana, the Slick Boys rode down on us. Since I was in my uniform, I thought they weren't going to mess with me. I was wrong. They made me take off my cover (hat), my coat, my jacket, and my shoes while they were searching me. They let me know that although I was in the marines, as far as they were concerned, I was still just a dope fiend.

A few days later, I went to Detroit to see Jeri and the kids. I had a nice visit with them, and on Friday, I returned to Chicago. On Sunday, I boarded a plane and flew to Augusta, Georgia. I caught a bus and rode to Ft. Gordon where I reported for duty. Monday, I started my training as a correctional specialist. However, by Friday, I was called into the Company Commander's office and told that I was being dropped from school because I didn't have a high school diploma or a G.E.D.

I was pissed. That was the second time that the military had done that to me. First the Army, now the Marines. They knew I didn't have a G.E.D. when I enlisted. There were only two other jobs left to choose from in the category I had chosen, supply or cook. I chose supply.

That night, I decided to go to Augusta with a white friend of mine to drink and party. While we were walking across the bridge, some "good ole boys" drove past us and bombarded us with raw eggs. They ruined my suede jacket that I had stolen from Poopy. That did it. I just wanted to get the hell out of Georgia.

I was Stationed in 22 Area in Camp Pendleton, California. I lived in a large barracks with individual cubicles that served as rooms. Everyone had their own television set, stereo, or whatever they could afford. Therefore, it was a very noisy living quarters. Before long, I was promoted to PFC (Private First Class).

The Marine Corp. was where I really learned about racial prejudice. It was prevalent on both sides. Being a black Marine at Camp Pendleton was like being a member of a private club. We wore tikkis around our necks. A tikki is several strands of black cords that are braded together and shaped like a cross at the end. We also wore them on our wrists. Whenever one of us entered the mess hall or passed other blacks on the streets, we greeted each other with raised, clenched fists. We also had a private handshake called, "dap," which was knocking our fists together. All white people were called "swines."

There was a real sense of black pride that I had never seen before, or since. black people did not fight each other, at least, not in public, and we didn't rip each other off. If a black person was walking down the rode or standing at a bus stop and a black man was driving by, he would stop and pick them up. Sometimes we would attend "Riffs." A Riff is where black people would get together and learn about our heritage.

As I learned about my heritage and my history, I started thinking about some of the things I had experienced and witnessed during my life. I thought about the civil rights struggle. I thought about the assassination of Dr. King and the Kennedy brothers. I thought about the racist policemen that patrolled our communities. All of a sudden, some of the things I had experienced started to make sense. It now made sense why some of my white schoolteachers didn't care whether I learned anything or not. It made sense why we were not allowed in certain neighborhoods. It made sense why many black people got fed up and started rioting in some of our major cities. Yes, it all made sense, now.

I became rebellious. One morning, during our daily inspection, I was starched, spit shined, and looking good as usual. I had always taken pride in how I looked. When the sergeant got to me, after checking out my uniform, boots, hair, and fingernails, he turned my belt buckle over. It wasn't shined, so he failed me. I became angry. No, I got mad. So I didn't shine it the next day either so he failed me again. Everyday I refused to shine the back of my belt buckle. After about a week of that, he wrote me up. When I went before the captain, I still hadn't shined it, and wasn't going to. I received a fine and a strong warning. So, I started shining the back of my belt buckle.

I was becoming more militant than military. I started beating up the white guys for no reason. It became a game to me. I was trying to see how many of them I could knock down with one punch. One day, I walked past a little white guy in the hallway, and I didn't like the way he looked at me. I hit him in his jaw but he didn't fall. While we were fighting, I gave him some of my best shots, but he still wouldn't fall down. Someone broke up the fight, but I felt like I had lost because this little bitty chump had stood toe to toe with me. My right hand was hurting, so I smoked a joint and went to bed.

The next day it was hurting really bad, so I went to the hospital. I found out I had broken some bones with one of the punches I had thrown the day before. I told the doctor I had broken them when I was punching the big bag in the gym. I told him that I wasn't wearing boxing gloves. He put a cast on it and assigned me to light duty.

One day I decided to start a race riot in the barracks. I called some of the brothers together and designed a strategic plan. Since we were grossly out numbered, about 10 to 1, we decided to wait until Friday night when most of the whites would be in town, partying in the bars. We would attack the unfortunate few that stayed behind.

There were two TV rooms in the barracks, one down stairs, and the other one up stairs. Since the downstairs one was next to the duty office, we decided to target the one up stairs. The plan was for all of the blacks to be in the down stairs TV room that night. That would force all of the whites to go up-stairs. Then, at a specified time, we would all walk in on them and start kicking behinds.

When Friday night rolled around, we put our plan into action. At 9:30, about ten of us walked into the TV room. I walked to the front of the room, turned the lights on, and the TV off. I stood in front of the TV and said, "OK gentlemen, we're taking over." I had read that in a book before and thought it sounded cool. I also wanted everyone to know who was in charge. I was making a statement. "Fear Me."

We attacked everyone in the room. I still had the cast on my arm and hand. I used it as a weapon. I held one of the guys down and savagely beat him over his head with it. When it was over we all ran out of the room and went our separate ways. I ran downstairs to my cube, took off my clothes, and got into bed. Ten minutes later, I heard a commotion down the hall. The M.P.s (military police) were going from cube to cube looking for people.

When they got to my cube they snatched me out of bed and told me to get dressed. They took me to the lock up on Main Side. Five of my cohorts were already there. I told them not to say anything to anyone. After we were all questioned, they let us go.

On Monday afternoon I was called to the colonel's office along with five of my co-defendants. We were lined up against the wall as the colonel walked past us. He told each of them they were going to jail. When he got to me, he stuck his finger in my face and said, "You are going to prison." He said that I was going to do 20 years.

I was put on restriction, pending trial. Restriction, a form of military house arrest, allows you to go to work, church, and the mess hall. Other than that, I was confined to the barracks. Since I couldn't go anywhere, I made the white men's lives miserable while they were in the barracks. I bought a tape by "The Last Poets," and blasted one particular poem called, "***The White Man's Got A God Complex***" over and over again. Every time someone tried to get me to turn the music down, I said, "If you don't want to hear it, leave."

After a couple of weeks I was tired of restriction and the marines. The only reason I enlisted was to keep from going to jail. Now, the Marines were trying to send me to prison, for twenty years. I decided it was time to leave. I said to myself, "I might be going to prison, but I'm going home to party first."

I hitchhiked to Ocean Side, caught the Greyhound to San Diego, and flew to Chicago from there. I tried to cover up the cast the best I could in case the M.P.s or the FBI were looking for me. That was a dead giveaway.

When I got to Chicago I took a cab to Ralph's. Gip was there and they were smoking weed and listening to music. I told them what happened and Gip cut the cast off my arm with one of his work tools. (He worked for the phone company.)

Michael and his girlfriend had moved to 16th and St. Louis. He had gotten a job as a cab driver. One night he told me that I could borrow his cab so I could make some money. I only picked up one fare the entire night; a couple with a small child. Everyone else looked like the stick-up man. After a few hours, I decided that driving a cab was not for me. I drove it back to Michael.

He decided to go back out to make some money. I asked him if he wanted me to ride along, but he said no. So, I crashed on the couch. Early the next morning, Michael's little sister, Peaches, was banging on the door. She told me that Mike had been shot in an attempted robbery and he was in the hospital. So was the guy that shot him. After Michael was shot, he took the man's gun, drug him out of the cab, and beat the hell out of him.

Sometimes I wonder what would have happened if I had been in the cab with Michael that night. Could I have prevented the shooting, or would we have both been shot? After a few days, Michael was released from the hospital. Before long, he was driving the cab again.

I was at Ralph and Debbie's one night when Red came by. We sat around drinking beer and smoking weed. Debbie didn't smoke weed, but she could put away some beer. We started getting the "munchies" so we decided to get something to eat. We bought chicken and more beer, and then headed back to Ralph's. When we stepped up on the porch, I had a piece of chicken in one hand, a cigarette in the other hand, and a joint behind my right ear. Ralph opened the door, paused, and stepped back out. He turned to me and said, "Hey man. You got company." The first thing I noticed was the official looking shoes inside the door.

Next, I noticed two, big, white men with badges. One of them asked me if I was Burton Barr. I started to say no, but I saw my picture in his hand. I knew they had to be FBI agents. I was wondering why they had come for me so soon. Normally, you had to be gone 30 days and declared a deserter before the FBI got involved. Maybe it was because of the seriousness of my case. Anyhow, I was busted.

I kept the right side of my face turned away from them so they wouldn't see the joint behind my ear. I asked if I could put my food down. I walked into the kitchen, took the joint from behind my ear, and hid it under a plate. I was thinking about how I was going to talk my way out of going to jail, when I heard them say that they were from the sheriff's department, and they had a warrant for my arrest for non-payment of child support.

I told them that I had an allotment going to my wife for my daughter. They asked me if I was in the military. I told them that I was in the Marines and that I was home on leave. I told them that I was shipping out to Vietnam the following week. It turned out that one of them was an ex-Marine. I showed him my I.D. and we started talking Marine talk (Semper Fi, and that kind of stuff).

He told me that he was supposed to take me in, but if I gave him my word as a Marine that I would go to headquarters the next day and straighten everything out, he would give me a break. I gave him my word and we shook on it.

That night, I caught the El train to Rose's house on 71st and State. She lived in a big apartment building that overlooked the Dan Ryan Expressway. Everyone called it, "50 West."

The next day, dad called instructing me not to come back to the west side. He said that some sheriff's police were looking for me and that they were really angry. I took his advice and stayed on the south side.

THE HOODLUM PREACHER

I hung out with Rose and her husband, Troy, and some of their friends that lived in the building. Butch came around and gave me some weed to sell so I could make some money, but I smoked it all up.

After about two months on the run, I decided to turn myself in and face the music. Troy took me to a place where I could surrender. When I walked in, they told me that the cells were too hot for anyone and to come back when the weather cooled down.

About a week later, I went to Fuzzy's house on Cermak and Lawndale. I hung out with him for a few days until I was ready to turn myself in again. So one Friday, at about midnight, Fuzzy and some of my other friends dropped me off in front of the place and gave me a joint to smuggle in. After they pulled off, I decided to smoke the joint before I went in. I walked down the street and stepped into a gangway so I could get the joint from my hiding place. When I stepped out, I noticed a car following me. I walked under a viaduct where the street was blocked off with a wire fence. I heard the car stop behind me. When I looked around, I saw a big white man walking towards me. Then the car pulled up to the other end of the viaduct and stopped. Another big white guy got out approaching me. I was trapped.

I still had the joint in my hand, so I started praying that they weren't the police. After realizing what neighborhood I was in, I started praying that they were the police. I stuck the joint in my mouth and started chewing it. When they got close to me, I backed against the wall and said, "What y'all want, man?" They flashed their badges and asked me where I was headed. I told them that I was AWOL from the marines and was turning myself in. They told me that I was walking in the wrong direction.

I told them that I was walking around because I wanted to enjoy a few more minutes of freedom before I went inside. They asked what I had been doing in the gangway, I told them that I had a joint and I wanted to smoke before I went in. They said that they knew it. They could smell it on me. They just wanted to see if I was going to tell them the truth. They asked me if I had anymore. I said no. Then they put me in the car and drove me to the M.P. station, wished me luck, and watched until I walked inside.

Inside, the sergeant said that it would be best if I went to Great Lakes Naval Station to turn myself in. That way, I wouldn't have to sit in a hot holdover cell for a week while I waited for someone to pick me up.

I couldn't believe it. For more than two months I had been sneaking and hiding, ducking and dodging, trying to stay out of jail. Now, I'd turned myself in twice, and both times they sent me away. They didn't know, however, that I was facing some very serious charges at Camp Pendleton. After that was found out, everything changed.

I waited until Sunday to go to Great Lakes. Since I had turned myself in, I stayed in a barracks instead of a cell, and I was free to walk around the base. On the plane, I sat in the front instead of the rear with the other prisoners. When we got to California, where the M.P.s knew me, it was just the opposite. I was the one who was chained and shackled. I spent the night in lock up. The next day I was taken to the brig, but since I had turned myself in, they decided to put me back on restriction.

I was taken back to 22 Area. When I walked in the mess hall, I received a hero's welcome from the other black Marines. They gave me a standing ovation and were holding up clenched fists. Some of them came over and gave me some dap. Since one of my chasers (prisoner escorts) was a friend of mine, I didn't have any problems.

While I was waiting for my court martial, I was on my best behavior. The Major that I was working for was so impressed with me that he volunteered to be a character witness for me at my trial. I was able to get a lot of character witnesses and a letter from U.S. Congressman Collins. By the time I went to trial, my court martial had been reduced from a general, where I could have been sentenced up to life, to a special, where the most I could get was six months.

My trial lasted two days. I found out that there was a witness that no one saw on the night of the assaults. He had seen us walking in and figured there was going to be trouble, so he lay down between some chairs that were directly behind me and the guy I had beaten. He saw everything, and was the prosecutions star witness.

THE HOODLUM PREACHER

There was another black Marine, nicknamed "Shorty," who had a cast on his arm the same time I did. I tried to use him to cast reasonable doubt on my guilt. It didn't work. They called him Shorty for a reason. I was found guilty of all charges.

Because of all of the influential people that stood up for me, and the way I carried myself in the courtroom and the months leading up to my trial, the judge saw me as a good person who had done one bad thing. He gave me the break of a lifetime. I was sentenced to two months of hard labor, reduced to the rank of Private and a forfeiture of two thirds of my pay for six months. The sentence was suspended, so all I had to do was stay out of trouble for six months. Fat chance.

Some of the brass (officers) were angry that I had gotten off so easily, so, they sent me as far away from 22 Area and main side as they could. I was transferred to a camp on the other side of the base called, Los Polgus, which was in 43 Area. I was assigned to Headquarters Platoon, Maintenance Company, 1st Service Battalion, 1st Marine Division.

I hated Los Polgus. It was in the boon docks, in the middle of nowhere. The movie theater was outside, like a drive in with benches. Sometimes there were snakes crawling around. There was only one club, and they only sold "near beer" and played country and western music. Worse of all, there were no women.

The only places where they sold real beer and liquor were in the NCO (non commissioned officers) clubs. I was 24 years old, but since I wasn't a corporal, I couldn't legally buy liquor on base. I had to resort to my teenage days when we used to get one of the old heads to buy liquor for us. In this case, sometimes the people that were buying liquor for me were younger than I was. But they were NCOs.

I made a few friends and was getting adjusted to the place. On payday weekends, I would rent a hotel room in Ocean Side, get a fifth of Johnny Walker Red and a lid (about an ounce) of reefer, and chill out. It was around that time that Congressman Collins was killed in a plane crash. He was headed to Chicago from Washington D.C. for the Christmas holiday. I was granted an emergency leave so I could attend his funeral. Although it was a sad occasion, it was good to be home without having to look over my shoulders for the police or the FBI.

I spent most of the time at Rose's crib at 50 West. One Saturday afternoon my mother called me and told me to get to Christiana as fast as I could. She said that Tadpole and Michael were killing each other. I don't know what she thought I could do. I didn't have a car, so it was going to take at least an hour to get there on the El and bus. But I had to get there. They were two of my best friends.

When I got to Christiana, Ralph, Gip, and Vernon were sitting in Butch's car, smoking weed and listening to War's new tape, "Gypsy Man". They told me that Michael had attacked Tadpole and stabbed him in the back with a butcher's knife. He left the knife in Tadpole's back and started walking away. That was a mistake, because Tadpole pulled the knife out of his back and cut Michael up real bad. They were both taken to the hospital, but they were o.k.

When I got back to Camp Pendleton I went back to my same routine, working during the day, and getting high at night. One night, while I was walking guard duty, I decided to take a break and get high. I saw, what looked like, a large metal crate. So I sat on it and lit a joint and a cigarette. When I finished smoking the joint, I stood up and reached for my rifle. When I bent down, I noticed a sign that was on the side of the crate. It was too dark out for me to see what it said, so I lit the cigarette lighter so I could see it better. It said, **"DANGER. NO SMOKING WITHIN 500 FEET."**

I closed the cigarette lighter and started moving away from the crate. I was so high, all I could do was laugh. I had always heard that God watches over fools and babies. I wasn't a baby, but He was sure watching over me.

A few weeks later, one of the brothers had taken some pills while he was on guard duty. He was too high to finish walking his post, so I took over for him so he wouldn't get into trouble. When I finished, I took some of the pills he had taken (I told you at the beginning of this book the mentality of the average drug user). I later found out that the pills were PCP. I had never been that high in my life.

THE HOODLUM PREACHER

Later that night, I found out that a white dude, named Skeet, had told on one of the brothers which got him into trouble. When Skeet got back to the barracks, I confronted him. He tried to walk away, but I wouldn't let him. I hit him in the jaw, knocking him down. I stood over him, yelling for him to get up. I wanted to knock him down again, but he wouldn't get up.

I started kicking him over and over again and telling him to get up. Skeet crawled on his back, trying to get away from my vicious kicks, but he backed himself against a wall. I don't know if it was the drugs or what, but all I saw was that bald, white, shining head, propped up against the wall. I picked up a G.I. can (a large garbage can) and started beating him in the head with it. On about the third or fourth blow, I missed his head and hit a water pipe that he was leaning against. I hit the pipe with such force, I broke it and water started shooting everywhere. Everyone started running, trying to get away from the water, and in the excitement, Skeet got away.

A few minutes later, Sergeant Wine, the duty sergeant for the day, came in. After they got the water stopped, he started asking everyone questions. When he got to me, I cursed him out and told him to mop up the water. He told me to go to bed, and I started talking about his mother. I eventually went to bed, but I laid there, cracking jokes and talking about Sergeant Wine's mother. That PCP had me on a roll, and I had the whole barracks laughing, even the white dudes, but the fun and games ended the next morning. The MPs came in and took me to the brig. Three months after my court martial, I was in trouble again.

The brig was a big secure building with lots of open dorms. The inmates called it, "The Hill" because of its location. Although it was just as racially divided, we all stuck together. It was no longer the blacks against the whites. It was the inmates against the establishment. But I quickly let everybody know where I stood. I didn't take no stuff out there, and I wasn't taking any in here either. I was held there pending my second special court martial.

They got us up early every morning and tried to make us do P.T. (physical training) like we were in boot camp, but most of us refused. We said, "What y'all going to do, put us in jail?"

88

Everyone had a job. Mine was working in the kitchen, washing dishes and mopping floors. During the evenings, we watched television or smoked weed that someone smuggled in.

When I went to court I was found guilty again. I was sentenced to six months hard labor, busted to private again, and forfeiture of two thirds of my pay for six months, but I didn't care. Life in the brig wasn't that bad.

One evening, the counselor called me to his office. He told me to call my father because he had been trying to reach me. I hadn't let my parents know what was going on because I didn't want them to worry. When I got dad on the phone, he told me that God had told him I was in trouble. We talked for a while and I assured him that I was all right. Then he prayed for me, and we hung up. After that, I started getting letters from dad almost every day.

I received a letter from someone else too. It was Jeri, telling me that we had a son. That was a shock to me because I didn't even know that she was pregnant. Besides that, I hadn't seen her in a year. Needless to say, that was the wrong time to get that letter.

One Friday afternoon, the guards tried to make the inmates that were in the yard come in early. They refused, and that started a riot. The whole brig was on lock down. We took over the brig. We covered up the cameras so the officers couldn't see what we were doing. We partied all weekend, staying up all night, watching TV and smoking weed.

Early Sunday evening, however, the party ended. There was a lot of noise outside, so we all went to the windows to see what was going on. The riot squad was out there with helmets, shields, tear gas, and dogs. We took our towels and wet them so we could cover our faces when they shot the tear gas in. We took all of the mattresses off the beds to use them as shields against the nightsticks. We made weapons out of everything we could find. Then we braced ourselves, and waited for the battle to begin. We knew we couldn't win, but we were determined to hurt some of them before they took us away.

When they got to the door, they offered us a deal. They said if we put our weapons down and surrendered, no one would be charged with anything and no one would get hurt. If we didn't, they were coming in to get us and we would all have a lot of time added to our sentences. It was fun while it lasted, but now the handwriting was on the wall. We surrendered.

Sometime later, I was sent to minimum custody. I was glad to get off of the hill. Being in minimum custody was almost like being free. We had all of the whiskey, beer, and drugs we wanted. We just couldn't leave.

After serving five months, I was released. I was taken back to 43 area and into the captain's office. He told me that he was going to give me another chance, but they weren't going to take any stuff off of me. I told him that I wasn't going to take any stuff off of them either, and if he wanted, they could take me back to the brig right then. He told me to get out of his office and think about my future as a Marine.

They gave me a few days off before I had to go back to work. I found out that the forfeiture of my pay wouldn't kick in until after my appeal was over, so I received the five months pay that had been held for me while I was incarcerated.

I went to Ocean Side and checked into a hotel. As usual, I bought a fifth of Johnny Walker Red, two six packs of beer, and a lid of reefer. The next day I went to a gun shop and purchased a 25 automatic pistol.

While I was in the brig, our company moved out of the quonset huts and into some brand new barracks near the offices, work areas, and mess hall. They were beautiful and modern. They almost looked like apartment complexes. The heads (toilets) and showers were inside the buildings, and most of the men had their own private rooms.

I was told they didn't have room for me in the new barracks. I had to live in one of the old quonest huts by myself. The good news was that I could choose whichever hut I wanted to live in, and whichever bed I wanted to sleep in. I had all the privacy I wanted, and I could hide my stash anywhere.

The bad news was that there was no electricity or heat. The head and showers were in a different building, and I was about three miles from everyone else. It was just the coyotes and me. I knew it was their way of punishing me, but I didn't care. They didn't want me around them and I didn't want to be around them. Screw them, all of them.

I kept my pistol on me at all times. It was small enough to carry in my pocket unnoticed. One day, during lunch break, one of the officers said that he wanted to search my belongings. When we got to my hut, he started searching my locker. He found the box that my pistol came in. I could tell from the expression on his face that he thought he had me. The box was empty. He asked me where the gun was that came in the box. I told him I had sent it home. He continued searching my locker, but he was disappointed when he didn't find anything. If he had searched me he would have found the gun. I guess he didn't think anyone was crazy enough to walk around the base with a gun in his pocket. He didn't know me.

After about a month they moved me to the new barracks with everyone else. For a while, I had my own room. I decorated it the best I could. I hung a lot of pictures of Pam Grier, both clothed and unclothed. To me, she was the finest woman in the world. The ceiling was paneled, so I hid my weed up there. After a couple of weeks they moved a roommate in with me. I was skeptical about him at first. I thought he might have been a CID officer (undercover police).

He was a Hispanic brother and I found out that he was all right. He was away a lot and he kept to himself. But just as we were getting to know each other, he was killed in an automobile accident.

I became friends with a couple of other guys in my building, Mitch, a brother from Mississippi, and Fat Freeman, a heavy-set white dude from Tennessee. They were really cool. I liked them. Freeman was the first of many of my white friends. I don't know how or when it happened, but I was no longer a militant or a racist. Maybe I never really was. Maybe I was just trying to fit in.

The three of us became running buddies. Freeman had a TV in his room, so we all hung out there, smoking weed, drinking whiskey, and watching TV. Sometimes, late at night, we would get the munchies. We would go down to the mess hall and sneak into the kitchen and steal food. Freeman was becoming disenfranchised with the Marines because the brass was hassling him about his weight.

That was also about the time that my appeal came back from my court-martial and the forfeitures started coming out of my paychecks. I had never been so broke in my life. I went from getting about $165.00 every other week to getting $15.00 every other week. I spent $10.00 of that on a lid (I had to have my weed), so that left me with $5.00 for everything else, including cigarettes.

That was during the same time that I received an emergency phone call from home notifying me that my father's brother, Uncle Bill, was dead. Before me, Uncle Bill had been the black sheep of the family. He had been into drugs for a long time. I found out later that he was always smoking weed in the basement and feeding the roaches (the butt of the joint) to our dog, Rex. That's probably why Rex acted so crazy. He was high. I'd also heard that he used to shoot heroin. Uncle Bill never let either Ralph or me know that he smoked weed and he never smoked with us until we were grown.

I wanted to go to Chicago for the funeral, but I didn't have any money. The Red Cross or Navy Relief would not help me because I was the source of my financial problems. So I had to hustle and scrape up the money the best way I could.

I made it to Chicago. When Ralph and I went around to say our last goodbyes, we put a joint in the casket under his pillow. I had to get back to California because I only had a five-day pass, and I didn't have much money.

After about four months I couldn't take it anymore. I was tired of being broke. I couldn't go into town. I couldn't buy anything (except weed). I was stealing soap from the PX (Post Exchange), so I could take a shower. They had won. I was beaten. They had finally broken me, literally. I vowed to myself that I would change my ways and try to make the best of the Marines.

I was given a job as requisitions clerk for Headquarters Platoon, meaning I placed the orders for all of the other platoons in Maintenance Company. My desk was located in a corner in the office, so I hung a sign above it that read, "THE CORNER BARR."

I got along well with my co-workers and with everyone else in the company. We formed touch football teams and played during our lunch breaks. The different platoons played against each other. On our team, Freeman was quarterback and I was the number one receiver. I was a good player and a fast runner but I had two problems. I dropped the ball a lot, and I didn't follow my blockers. Sometimes Freeman would call a play that was designed for me to get the ball and run to the right. But if I didn't like the way things looked, I ran to the left instead. The problem was my blockers, who were my protection, were going to the right. But I thought that I was fast enough to make it on my own. So I went in the other direction.

Sometimes God sets up "blockers" to protect us and pave the way for us. The blockers might be our parents, our pastors, or our teachers. The problem is, sometimes we don't like the way things look or what they tell us. So instead of following them, we go in the other direction, thinking that we are smart enough to make it on our own. Although we played touch football, there was a lot of physical contact and we played on concrete. Almost everyday someone left the field battered, bruised, or bleeding, but it was fun, and we loved to play.

The brass started noticing the change in my attitude and my work ethics. I never waited for anyone to tell me what to do. If there was something that needed to be done, I just did it. If there was nothing to do, I picked up a broom and started sweeping.

My platoon sergeant, Staff Sergeant Green, was transferred and replaced with Gunnery Sergeant Martinez. I really liked S/Sgt. Green. He had a lot to do with my change of attitude. He pushed me sometimes and made me angry, but he was just trying to help me to reach my potential. He was the one who recommended that I be promoted to PFC, again. I really hated to see him go.

Later, I found out that Gunny Martinez was just as cool. He was a good person to work for, and we got along really well. He was very funny too. Whenever we asked him something, his favorite saying was, "I don't know, and I don't want to know."

It wasn't long before Gunny told me that he was recommending me for a meritorious promotion to Lance Corporal. A meritorious promotion is when you go before a panel of staff

NCOs and are questioned about your knowledge of the guidebook for Marines. It is meritorious because you don't have to wait the required length of time to be promoted.

I went before the panel, but I blew the questions about the phonetic alphabet. Phonetic alphabet is using words instead of letters, such as: Alpha, Bravo, Charlie instead of ABC. So, I didn't get the promotion. The following month, Gunny recommended me again and once again, I blew the phonetic alphabet.

Gunny told me that he was going to recommend me again the following month, and I'd better make it that time. I wondered why it was so important to Gunny that I was promoted. I found out that it wasn't just Gunny. The whole company was rooting for me, from the company commander on down. Even Sgt. Wine, whose testimony sent me to the brig a few months earlier, supported the recommendation.

I was starting to feel the pressure but I was determined to make it this time. I had always done well on all of the questions except the ones that dealt with the phonetic alphabet, so that was what I focused on. I recorded the alphabet on tape and let it play all night while I was sleeping. I even slowed down on smoking weed (temporarily), so I could keep my mind clear. When the day came, I was ready.

The panel met in the First Sergeant's office as usual. The First Sergeant was the highest-ranking enlisted person in the company. He was also the highest-ranking black person I had known, and was one of my strongest supporters and my role model. He was an example of what I could be if I kept my nose clean and put my mind to it.

When the questioning started, I answered them with confidence and clarity. They asked, "What is your first general order?" I answered, "Sir. My first general order is, to walk my post in a military manner, keeping always on the alert and observing everything within sight or hearing." The questioning went on for about ten minutes; I was on a roll.

Then came the phonetic alphabet. They asked, "What is the phonetic alphabet for L?" I answered, "Sir. The phonetic alphabet for L is Lima." I went on, answering alphabet after alphabet until it was over. The first sergeant asked me to step outside while the panel conferred. When I was called back in, he congratulated me and told me that I was the first person in company history to answer every question correctly.

The following week during morning formation, I was officially promoted to lance corporal but the celebration didn't last long. Gunny told me that he was recommending me for another meritorious promotion. The following month, I went before the panel again. Just like before, I aced the questions and I was promoted to corporal. In just a four month period, I went from private to corporal. I hadn't been out of the brig a year, and there I was, Corporal Burton Barr Jr. Non-Commissioned Officer.

Gunny Martinez had done a lot for me. Not only did he help me reach the rank of corporal, but he also kept me from being sent overseas. Every time I received orders to go somewhere, he got them cancelled. He would say, "You're not going anywhere, Barr. You're staying right here with the rest of us." And I did.

Eventually, however, things changed. Gunny retired and the First Sergeant was transferred to Main Side. Mitch and Freeman finished their stints and were discharged. My crew was gone but, I quickly made new friends. There was Harris, a sergeant from Macon, Georgia; Brother Williams from Erie, Pennsylvania; Andretti, a brother from Boston; Figueroa, a Hispanic brother; and a white brother, named Steve.

Andretti lived in Ocean Side with his wife, a very sweet white woman named Laura. We often hung out at their house, drinking, smoking weed, and socializing. Andretti's favorite TV program was "Sanford and Son," and he was very good at imitating Redd Fox.

We were always playing jokes on each other, but one day they got me good. We had been smoking a lot of weed, and I had the munchies real bad. Andretti said that all he had to eat was some chocolate candy. I ate all of it. I was wondering why everyone was laughing, until I found out it was not chocolate candy I had eaten; It was Exlax. I spent the rest of the day and night, sitting on the toilet.

One day, I was told that I was going to be part of a group that would be participating in two weeks of war games. We would be on a ship for the first week, and in the field the second week.

One night, while we were on the ship, some of us decided to go up on deck and smoke some weed. The ship was out in the ocean, and we were on a "Blackout," meaning all of the lights were turned off, so that the enemy wouldn't see us. It was so dark we literally couldn't see our hands in front of our faces. When we finished getting high, I staggered around, trying to find the hatch (door) that we came in. When I finally found it, I went downstairs and went to bed.

The next morning, the brass called everyone to the flight deck. They found evidence that someone had been smoking weed on deck the previous night. It turned out that, because of the darkness, we had gone to the wrong deck. We didn't know that we were on the flight deck. That was the most dangerous place to be, especially at night, during a Blackout, because there were no guardrails on one side. While I was staggering around trying to find the hatch, I could have walked right off of the ship. Oh! I forgot to mention something. I couldn't swim. So, I would have been in real trouble.

When the first week was over, we climbed down the side of the ship on nets and got into "Mike Boats." The Mike Boats took us to the shore where we attacked the beach, assimilating an amphibious landing in enemy territory. After we landed, we went to the field where the war games were taking place. Anyone who was tagged (wounded or killed), was supposed to go back on the ship and come off again as reinforcements. If anyone tried to tag me, they were going to have a real fight on their hands because I was not getting back on that ship. Period.

We lived in the field all week and slept in tents. At least, we were supposed to sleep in the tents. Harris and I shared a tent, but we never slept in it. Every night, after dark, we would sneak out to the edge of camp where Andretti would be waiting in his car. Then we would go to his house to drink and smoke weed. He would drop us off the next morning before sunrise. We did that all week long.

I was glad when all of that was over, and I was able to get back to my regular routine. A few of us went to San Diego that weekend to party. That had been one of my regular hangouts before my first court-martial. During that time, I was known as

"Cool Breeze." My friends called me that because they said that I was "too cool to move." It had been a while since I had been there.

We were at one of the local nightclubs, dancing and having a good time, when I saw a cute young lady sitting at one of the tables. I went over to her and asked her to dance. It was a slow song, so while we were dancing, we had a chance to talk. She said her name was Ann, and she lived in San Diego. When she asked what my name was, I told her it was Bob. Bob had been one of my father's nicknames. I didn't give her my real name because I didn't think I would ever see her again. We ended up dancing several times and later exchanging phone numbers. Since I lived in the barracks, I gave her my work number.

She called me a few days later and invited me to come to San Diego to see her. I decided to go the next day. Since I didn't have a car, I asked Andretti to take me. We drove down after work that evening.

San Diego is approximately 40 miles from Camp Pendleton. We picked up some beer and wine on the way and arrived at Ann's at about 7 o'clock. We all sat and talked for a while, but after about an hour or so, I told Andretti to go on home and leave me there. Both he and Ann seemed to be shocked at that statement. To be honest, I was too. I didn't have a clue as to how I was going to get back to the base without a car.

After Andretti left, Ann and I started getting more intimate. I spent the night with her and caught a cab to the Greyhound Bus Station the next morning. Over the next few weeks I made the trip to San Diego several times to see her. Eventually, I packed my stuff and moved in with her while maintaining my room in the barracks. Afterwards, I got a loan from the credit union and bought a used car; a red 1971 Chevy Camaro with a black vinyl top.

Ann had a small, two bedroom apartment in a building on 61st street that resembled the one on the TV program, "Three's Company." She had a son and a daughter who lived with her. She also had several sisters; most of them lived in San Diego. Her parents lived there too. Her youngest sister, Gwen, lived in Compton with her daughter.

Gwen was my favorite. She was the one that was closest to my age, and we had a lot in common. I had always wanted to learn how to play the flute, and she had one. She taught me the basics and let me keep it for as long as I wanted. We hung out together a lot and we enjoyed some of the same things. If I hadn't been already dating Ann, I probably would have gone after Gwen. Ann was a couple of years older than I was but that didn't matter. I had dated older women before.

After I moved to San Diego, some of my friends followed suit. Harris started dating one of Ann's friends, Kay, and moved in upstairs with her. Steve started dating the apartment manager, who lived next door, and moved in with her. Williams met a young lady that lived on the other side of San Diego and moved in with her.

There was a white couple that lived in the apartment next to ours. Since theirs was the front apartment, they could see the street. At about 2 or 3 o'clock one morning, we were awakened by them banging on the wall. They told us that someone was outside, stealing our tires. I grabbed my gun and went outside and Ann called upstairs for Harris. When I got outside, I saw my car jacked up, and a man kneeling next to it. When he saw me coming, he jumped in his car and drove off. I fired several shots at him as he sped away.

By that time, Harris, Kay, and Ann came out. Harris was helping me put the tires back on the car while Ann and Kay were standing there, talking. All of a sudden, I heard Kay yell, "Watch out," and she and Ann started running toward the building. When I looked up, I saw the tire thief's car coming toward us. When he got close, he started shooting at us. I grabbed my gun and returned fire. After a few seconds, he drove off. I was glad he did, because I was out of bullets. I ran in the house, reloaded, and went back out, but he didn't come back. The next day, the couple that lived in the front apartment moved out. About a week later, Andretti and Laura moved in.

CHAPTER FIVE

The Hoodlum

Ann never took part in any of my criminal activities. She smoked weed sometimes, but so did almost everybody else in those days. She worked very hard at being a good mother to her children.

However, she was instrumental in hooking me up with some people that I needed to know. One of them was her brother-in-law, Thad. Thad was one of the major players in San Diego's street life. I first met him when I was looking for some weed. He had a lot of connections, so I was able to buy kilos of marijuana, sell some, and make my money back. A kilo is two pounds and two ounces, and cost between $145.00 and $165.00. Kilos were called, "keys" or "bricks," because they were packed so tightly, they looked like bricks.

Weed was cheaper in San Diego because it was next to the Mexican border. The farther away you went, the higher the cost. So I started shipping kilos to Ralph, in Chicago, where I could triple my money.

Whenever someone that was from the east coast, or Midwest, was getting out of the Marines, they wanted to take a kilo or two home with them. For a fee, I would get them what they wanted. Thad and I came up with an idea that would allow us to make 100% profit. We started ripping people off.

Thad and I started putting together our own bricks. They were composed of newspaper, grass from someone's lawn, and a small amount of high quality weed that was strategically placed for testing purposes.

We chose our vics (victims) carefully. They were servicemen who had been discharged and wanted to use some of their separation pay to buy some bricks to take home. They were usually from the East Coast or Midwest, and we always waited until they were ready to go to the airport before we made our move. That way, time was on our side. I always played the part of the middleman. I rode with the vics, collected the money, and made the transactions. I would caution them not to open the brick because it was packaged in a way that the dogs couldn't detect it. If they wanted to test it, I would cut a small hole where we had placed the real weed. After they tested it, I would seal it back up, and they would stash it in their duffle bags with the rest of their gear.

Since airport security wasn't very tight back then, especially for military personnel, they had no problems getting through. The best thing about this con was by the time the vics realized that they had been take,; they were thousands of miles away.

Thad and I ran that scam so many times, I was starting to become quite an actor. Little did I know that the time would soon come when I would have to give the performance of my life.

One day, one of the brothers in my platoon that was from Philadelphia told me that he and two other brothers were getting out at the same time. Between them, they wanted 12 kilos. He asked if they could get a discount since they were buying so much. I assured him that something could be worked out. I called Thad and we set up the sting.

I told them that the price was $1400.00. They gave me the money and one of them rode with me to Thad's. I acted like I was buying two bricks for myself. After I made the transaction, we went back to the spot where the others were waiting. Before I could stop him, one of them opened one of his packages. When he saw what was in it, he showed it to the others, and they opened theirs too. I knew that my life was in danger, and I had no choice but to play the game all the way out. So I opened one of my packages and acted like I was just as angry as they were.

To play it off, I called Thad and told him what was in the packages. When I got off of the phone, I told them that Thad was calling his suppliers to try to straighten everything out. They started calling some of their friends, and before I knew it, there were about a half dozen dudes there with pistols, rifles, and shotguns, and we were all ready to ride down on Thad. I acted like I was going to get my pistol, but the truth is, I'd already had it. I just needed time to let Thad know what was happening. He called some of his people, and they were ready and waiting for us. There were three cars of us headed to Thad's for a show down, and there I was, caught in the middle.

When we got to Thad's, he was standing on the front porch. I told everyone to wait in the car while I talked to him. While I was walking towards him, I was real nervous. I didn't know how this thing was going to play out. One of Thad's hands was behind his back and I knew his gun was in it. I had my gun in my hand too.

I saw some of Thad's boys in the window with their rifles and shotguns. I remember thinking to myself, suppose someone starts shooting? Who am I going to shoot at, and who will be shooting at me?

I knew I had to convince Thad that I hadn't taken sides with the dudes in the cars, and at the same time, I couldn't let the men in the cars know that Thad and I were partners. But most of all, I couldn't let anybody see me sweat.

When I got to the porch, Thad said, "We can't give any money back." I already knew that. One of the first things I had learned about the con game was, never give the money back. I was just trying to figure out how to keep it, and at the same time, avoid a bloody gunfight.

We came up with a plan. Thad went in the house and brought out several bricks that we had made up earlier. He told everyone (me included) that those were some of the packages that he had picked up along with ours. He didn't know that they were bogus packages until I had called him. He said he didn't have any money to give back because he had been ripped off too. Since we all had lost money, it would be senseless for us to kill each other.

But to draw suspicion away from my self, I acted like I didn't want to hear anything that Thad was saying. I still wanted my money. But after discussing it for a few minutes, I let them believe that they had convinced me to just let it go.

While we were riding away, I apologized to them for losing all of their money. They said it wasn't my fault and there were no hard feelings. I took them to the airport. When we got there, we hugged and wished each other well, and I watched them get on the plane. Then I drove back to Thad's house and picked up my $700.00.

Ann and I were not exactly rolling in money, but between my military pay and my hustling we were doing OK. She got a job and we went from a no-car family to a two-car family. We even had a small bank account. Things were going well on the base too. The four of us, Harris, Andretti, Williams, and I rode to the base together everyday. We took turns driving. The only problem was, for some reason, I kept getting speeding tickets. No one else did.

Thad got arrested for something and went to jail, so I had to come up with a new hustle. I bought a gram of cocaine and tried selling it but there were not a lot of people who wanted to pay $25.00 for a bag of coke.

Williams had a couple of dudes selling weed for him on base. He was doing OK, but he needed a partner. So he asked me to go into business with him. The way it worked was, he would give each of them a package of thirteen lids. Each lid sold for $10.00. On payday, they had to pay him for ten lids. Therefore, the dealers made $30.00 off of each package. I had to give it to him, it was a great plan.

I was able to get the bricks at a lower price than Williams, so we were able to increase our profit margin. I also convinced some of the contacts I made while I was in the brig to work for us. Within two weeks, we went from having two dealers to having eight dealers on our payroll. After a while, we increased the number of lids we gave to some of the dealers. There were three levels. We gave the level one dealers thirteen bags, and they owed us $100.00. We gave the level two dealers twenty-six bags, and they owed us $200.00. The level three dealers received thirty-nine bags, and they owed us $300.00. Most of the dealers sold their bags on credit. Since everybody got paid on the same day, they didn't have any trouble collecting their money and neither did we.

Business was so good, that some nights it took us all night to bag up the lids to deliver to our dealers. I would wait until Ann and the kids went to bed, and then Williams would come over, and the kitchen floor would literally be filled with marijuana.

We brought on a few more dealers, so we were making some pretty good money. I was starting to miss the thrill of the con. This might sound crazy to some people, but there is something about the danger of living on the edge that is intriguing to people in that lifestyle. Maybe that's why they call it a con "game." To the players, it is a game, a very serious game. If you win, you have the satisfaction of knowing that you've outsmarted some of the most intelligent people in the world: doctors, lawyers, bankers, judges, policemen, merchants, and even other hustlers. If you lose, you can lose more than just your money. You can lose your freedom, or even your life. As they say, that's the game. Everybody can't play it, but if you choose to try, you'd better be prepared to face the consequences if you lose; and those consequences can be severe.

That kind of lifestyle makes perfectly good sense when you are living outside the will of God. We cannot see God's truths because we are blinded by Satan's lies and his promises of fame and fortune. God wants us to live abundantly, but we choose to listen to the one who has come to steal, to kill, and to destroy. *John 10:10*

I taught Williams the game that Thad and I had played for so long. We started selling fake kilos to unsuspecting servicemen that were going home but we took it a step further. Williams found an apartment building with a back door in the hallway that led to an alley. I played the straight man, meaning, I rode with the vic. When we got to the spot, I would get the money and go into the building. Then I would go out the back door and into the alley where Williams was waiting in his car. We would drive away and split the money. We ran that con over and over again, and it worked every time. Eventually, we had so many people dealing for us, we were rolling in dough.

My mother came out to California to visit us for a couple of weeks. We took her on a couple of tours throughout the state and to Mexico. She had an old friend that was living in Los Angeles, so we took her to see him. Williams rode with us so we could take care of business while we were there.

Mother's friend had a big house that was nicely decorated. What she didn't know was that her friend smoked weed. We took advantage of that fact by bringing him on as one of our dealers. That opened up a whole new market for us and he brought in a lot of business.

There was another brother that worked for our company. His name was Cody. We got high every once in a while, but we never really hung out together. We hooked up one evening after work and went bar hopping. After a couple of hours, we went to one of his friend's crib. They started cooking some boy (heroin) and asked me if I wanted any. It had been a long time since I had stuck a needle in my arm, but I did it anyway. When I got home, Ann instinctively knew there was something wrong with me, but I didn't tell her what was happening. Cody and I never hung out again after I found out that he was strung out on boy; I didn't want to go back to that lifestyle.

Our landlord's sister lived in the apartment directly above ours. Her name was Toni and she was a very beautiful woman who just happened to be white. Her apartment was between Kay's and Jim's, another friend of mine. One evening, Harris and Kay were out, so I went to Jim's apartment to hang out with him for a while. As I was leaving, I saw Toni standing on her porch.

We started talking, and before I knew it, we were in her apartment, and then, in her bedroom. After we finished our business, I was about to leave but heard Harris and Kay coming up the stairs. I decided to wait until they went inside and closed the door, and then sneak down the stairs. Instead of staying in the house, however, they went back downstairs and sat on the steps. Before long, everyone in the building was sitting out front, including Ann.

Oh! I forgot to mention something. None of the apartments had back doors. The only way out was to walk down the front stairs, which happened to be where every occupant of the building was sitting. That is, everyone except Toni and me. I was trapped. There was no way out. If that wasn't bad enough, my car was still in the driveway.

I called Williams and told him what was going on. Then I called Ann and told her that Williams had picked me up and I was at his house. I sat in Toni's, trying to wait for everyone to go in the house. It was close to midnight, and they were still out there, so I went to sleep.

I woke up at about 3:00 a.m. and decided to make my move. I went onto the porch and peeked down the stairs. The coast was clear. I started tiptoeing down the steps very slowly. When I got about halfway down, I heard Ann hollering, "You ain't got to tip. I know you're up there." I was busted. She had sat under the steps all night, waiting for me to come out.

We argued for a while, and then I went to work. When I got home that evening, I found out that Ann had broken Toni's windows and Toni had moved because she didn't know what else Ann might do. Everyone was mad at me, but I later learned why the men in the building were so angry. It seemed that I wasn't the only one that was "visiting" Toni. Now, because of me, she was gone.

That night, and for the next few weeks, when we went to bed, I made sure that I was holding Ann in my arms when I went to sleep. It wasn't that I was trying to be intimate. I was just making sure that I woke up every time she moved. I'd heard about that "woman scorned" stuff, and I wasn't taking any chances.

I put in for a transfer to 22 Area. I thought it might be fun to go back to Main Side since I was an NCO. I was wrong. I no longer had the freedom to roam around as I pleased. I was stuck at a desk in a room with a setup resembling a classroom. The platoon sergeant was a racist master sergeant whose desk was in the front of the room facing us, like the teacher facing his students. I hated that, and it showed.

I started showing up late for work. Sometimes I just didn't go in at all. Although I was assigned to 22 Area, technically I was still in Maintenance Company. I was just on loan to them. So, there were times that the brass in 22 Area thought I was in 43 Area, and the brass in 43 Area thought I was in 22 Area. When in reality, I was at home in San Diego getting high. The platoon sergeant made it clear that he didn't like me, but I didn't care since I didn't like him either.

There was a drought on weed in southern California. No one could find any anywhere. After a few weeks, things were beginning to get desperate. I met a white couple through Ann that had a lot of connections. We used them from time to time to notarize false documents. We called them to see if they knew of anyone who had something. A few days later, they called and told us they had found someone who could get us all the weed we wanted.

Because of the drought, we decided to get as much of the weed as we could. Ann didn't know it, but I cleaned out our bank account, and so did Williams. Between the two of us, we had over $5000.00. We were going to make a killing.

THE HOODLUM PREACHER

We arranged to meet them one Saturday morning at a Denny's restaurant in Carlsbad. Williams and I got there early, so we got some coffee and waited. The connection got there about ten minutes later. They were two regular looking white dudes. They said that they had to go and get the weed, but only one of us could go with them. Since we had come in Williams' car, we decided that he should go. They said that they would be back in a half hour. They got into Williams' car and left. I sat in the booth, sipping on coffee and waiting.

After about an hour, I knew something was wrong. All kinds of thoughts ran through my mind. Did they kill Williams and take the money? I started pacing the floor. About thirty minutes later, Williams walked in. The look on his face spelled bad news.

He said that when they got to the spot, they told him to wait in the car while they went in. We had run that game too many times, on too many people, to fall for that one. Williams said that one of them had to wait in the car with him. He told me that one of the guys went in and the other one stayed in the car. They waited for approximately an hour, but the other guy never came back. I asked him where the guy who stayed with him in the car was. He said, "He's in the trunk."

We drove to a deserted area and beat the heck out of the dude in the trunk. Williams wanted to kill him and throw him in the ocean. I wanted to kill him too, but that wasn't going to get our money back. I called his mother and told her that we were going to kill her son if we didn't get our money. She said that she would pay us, but we decided not to take that chance. She might have the police or FBI waiting for us. Then we would have a kidnapping case.

We made him tell us where the car was that he and his partner came in. It was an old, beat up van. We went to our connection that had led us to this dude and his partner in the first place. We told them what had happened. We made the dude sign his van over to me, and our friends notarized it. We kept him bound and gagged, and in the car trunk all night and the next day. Williams still wanted to kill him. Finally, late that Sunday night, we took him to a deserted area and let him go.

Ann didn't know that I had lost all of our money, and I didn't want her to know. So I had to get some money fast. We went on a two day, armed robbery spree. I had never robbed anyone before (or since), but I was desperate. By the time we were done, we had the money we had lost, plus some.

We made a lot of fast money robbing people, but I really didn't like doing it. First, there was no challenge in it. Anybody can stick a gun in someone's face and say, "Give it up," but it takes somebody that's really special, to be able to talk to someone and make them want to give them their money. The second thing I didn't like about robbing people was the look on their faces, the look of fear and terror. No, robbery was not for me.

As I stated earlier, I was officially a part of Maintenance Company in 43 Area. So when I became eligible to be promoted to sergeant, I put in my bid. The company commander and the rest of the brass still saw me as the sharp Marine that turned his life around, so they signed off on the promotion. I knew I had to keep my advancement a secret from the brass in 22 Area until everything was final, or the platoon sergeant would block my promotion.

It worked and I got my promotion. It became official during morning formation. I was called forward by the company commander and given my sergeant stripes. I went to one of my friend's room in the barracks and changed into a shirt that I had left there earlier. The shirt already had the sergeant stripes sewn on.

When I walked into the office in 22 Area, late as usual, some of the brothers saw my new stripes and started to congratulate me. The platoon sergeant saw them too, and he called me to his desk. He asked me why I was wearing sergeant stripes. I said, "Because I'm a sergeant." He said he hadn't recommended me for a promotion. I told him that he didn't have to.

I could see the anger on his face. I had beaten him, and he didn't like it. He said, "OK, Slick. You got your stripes. Now let's see how long you keep them." He was giving me a warning. I should have listened, but I was too cocky.

Look what I had accomplished. Three years ago, I was a junkie walking the streets of Chicago. Less than two years ago, I was sitting in a cell in the brig. Now, I was a sergeant in the toughest, most respected branch of the armed forces, the United States Marine Corp.

I didn't know it at the time, but I was at a crossroad in my life. I could straighten up, take charge of my destiny, and be all I could be, or I could continue down that path of destruction that I seemed to love so much. It wasn't long before the decision was made for me.

I knew that what I was doing was wrong. Deep down inside, I wanted to change the direction of where I was going. I knew that I was heading some place that I didn't want to go. The problem was that I had gotten too comfortable in that lifestyle. It is like riding on a nice, warm bus on a cold winter day. All of a sudden, you realize that you are on the wrong bus. The bus that you are on is headed downtown, but that is not where you want to go. You know you should get off, but it is so cozy and comfortable that you decide to ride just a little while longer. You might even doze off for a while. Before you know it, you're at the end of the line. You are in the heart of downtown because you didn't get off of the bus when you had a chance.

There are a lot of men and women who are on the wrong bus. Satan is the driver, and he is taking them someplace they don't want to go. He's taking some of them to the penitentiary. He's taking some of them to the cemetery. He's taking some of them to the very pits of hell. They know that they are going the wrong way, but they are so comfortable that they want to ride just a little longer. God is steadily saying to them, "Get off of the bus."

There was a big inspection coming up. The platoon sergeant asked me to take some of the men into town so they could pick up their uniforms from the cleaners. Since I wanted to get out of the office anyway, I did it. On our way back, my car was stopped at the gate. I was told to pull over. When I did, I saw an M.P. (Military Police) walking toward us with a dog. We were told to get out of the car.

After we got out, we were all searched. The M.P.'s searched under the hood (where I usually hid my stash) and the interior of the car. The dog was trained to find marijuana, but he didn't find any. During the search, I was worried about them finding my gun hidden under the dashboard behind some wires. When they didn't find it, I was relieved.

I knew that I had been set up. The brass had known for some time that Williams and I were dealing weed, but they couldn't catch us. I was feeling cocky because I thought I had beaten them again. They had picked the wrong time to stop me. The only illegal thing that was in my car was my gun, and they didn't find it.

Finally, the officer told me to open the trunk. I just knew that the search was practically over, because I never kept anything in the trunk. When I opened it, I saw my field jacket that I had been looking for. I remember thinking to myself, "Oh! That's where my jacket is." But then, I remembered what was in my jacket, a tobacco pouch containing six, quarter ($25.00) bags of cocaine.

I wasn't feeling cocky anymore, but I tried not to lose my composure. I started praying, "Lord, please don't let him find the pouch." He pulled the pouch out of the pocket. I started praying, "Lord, please don't let him open the pouch." He opened the pouch and looked in it. I started praying, "Lord, please don't let the cocaine be in there." He reached into the pouch and pulled out the bags of cocaine. He showed them to me and asked what they were. I said, "I don't know. You got it." I was arrested and taken to the lock-up at main side. I was processed and then released, pending charges.

Eventually, I was transferred back to 43 Area, but things were not the same. Most of my friends, including Harris and Andretti had finished their military obligations and were discharged, but I was glad they stayed in San Diego. Williams and I continued doing business as usual. As I look back, it was about that time that I started losing control. It was almost like I didn't care anymore. I was coming to the realization that life, as I had known it, would soon be over.

One day, one of Williams' friends asked me to get him two kilos. I told him that they would cost $150.00 each. I thought he would go with me to cop them, but he just gave me the money. I decided to rip him off. Normally, I didn't operate that way. I never ripped off anyone that I knew, or that wasn't being discharged and leaving town.

The next day, he came to my house, demanding that I give him his money. I told him I didn't have it. I had been ripped off, and it was his fault because he wasn't with me. He wasn't trying to hear that. He started threatening me, and that was the wrong thing to do in my house. I started walking into my bedroom and he followed me. That was just what I'd wanted him to do. I reached in the dresser drawer and pulled out my pistol. I cocked it and put it against his head. I told him that if he didn't get out of my house I was going to blow his head off. He knew that I meant it. He looked at me and said, "This ain't over." Then he left.

My ripping off Williams' friend put a strain on our relationship. I didn't know that they were that close. It was obvious that he didn't approve of what I had done, but I couldn't change it. I had learned something when I first started in the con game with Thad - never give the money back, period.

I received a sad phone call from my mother one day. She told me that my friend, Michael, was dead. They think that the same person that had killed his brother, Huckabuck, had shot and killed him too. I was very sad to hear that. Michael and I had gone through a lot together.

I found out that I was going to be court-martialed for the cocaine that was found in my car. The brass did everything they could to make my life a living hell. So, I became rebellious again. They took my job and had me just sitting around, doing nothing all day. I was given menial assignments and had to run a lot of errands. They tried to force me to move back on base, but I refused.

I missed work every chance I got. When I did go, I was late. One day, Captain Rice, the company commander, called me in to his office. He told me that if I were late again, he would lock me up. He said, "If your car breaks down on the highway, you'd better jump out and start running."

One morning, I overslept after partying too hard the night before. When I saw what time it was I knew that I was going to be late. I got dressed, went outside, raised the hood of the car and poured some gas in the carburetor. Then I lit a match and set it on fire. When it started burning, I went inside and called the fire department. After they put the fire out, I borrowed Andretti's car and went to work. I was about three hours late.

They assigned a military lawyer to me, but I hired a private attorney. I didn't trust them anymore because I knew they were out to get me. How did I know that? They told me. The company commander, the platoon commander, and the platoon sergeant let me know that I was a disgrace to the Marines, and they wanted me out.

My attorneys called me in with good and bad news. The good news was, the charges didn't warrant a general court-martial, so they got it reduced to a special court, my third one. In a special court-martial, the maximum punishment I could get was six months confinement and a bad conduct discharge. The bad news was, I would probably be convicted and given the maximum sentence, because Colonel Anderson, the division commander, had heard of me, and he wanted me out of his Marine Corp.

I also found out that they were adding U.A. (Unauthorized Absence) to the charges against me, because I was three hours late for work on the day that my car caught fire. The Army calls it, AWOL. That way, if I was able to beat the drug charges, they could still get me for something. I decided that I was not going down without a fight.

One of my running buddies was a dude named Figueroa who stayed in almost as much trouble as I did. As a matter of fact, he was U.A. at the time of my trial. I convinced him to testify on my behalf by saying that the cocaine found in my car was his. He was going to say that I had loaned him my field jacket, and when he returned it, he had accidentally left the drugs in it. I convinced several other men to testify that they saw Figueroa give me the jacket on the morning that I was arrested, and they saw me put it in the trunk of the car. I went to the fire department and got a copy of the report that was filed on the morning that my car caught fire. By the time my trial was to start, I was ready.

My trial lasted two days. The jury consisted of four staff NCOs from my division, including one from my company. The prosecution presented their case first. They told the jury how I was caught red handed with the drugs in my car. They pressed the point of my being irresponsible, because I was three hours late reporting to my assignment on the day I was written up.

When my attorneys presented my case, I was not impressed. They did OK, but I got the impression that they were not giving it their best. My attorneys never introduced the letter from the fire department into evidence. They said that it wouldn't do any good.

Although Figueroa was U.A., he was able to sneak into court, testify, and sneak back out without being caught. My other witnesses did well too. I thought things were going great until the prosecution called in my company commander, my platoon commander, and my platoon sergeant as rebuttal witnesses. They all said basically the same thing. I was a known liar, and so were all of my witnesses. I was found guilty on all counts and sentenced to six months hard labor, reduced to the rank of private, again, and given a bad conduct discharge. They had finally gotten me.

By the time court adjourned, it was almost 10:00 PM. I was handcuffed and put in a jeep. Instead of heading to the brig, the driver took me to 43 Area. He said that Captain Rice, the company commander, was waiting at headquarters to see me. When we got there, all of the office buildings were closed down and locked up. There was only one light on in the entire area. That was the one in Captain Rice's office.

When I was taken to his office, I stood there handcuffed, and he stood there gloating. He said, "I told you that I was going to get you, Private Barr. I finally got you out of my Marine Corp." Then he snatched the insignia (plastic sergeant stripes) off of my field jacket and said, "You won't be needing these anymore." I reminded him that I had bought and paid for those stripes at the PX, and I wanted them back. He put the stripes in my pocket and said to the guard, "Get this trash out of here." They put me back in the jeep and took me to the brig.

When I got there, I was told that they would have to put me in P.C. (protective custody) because I was a sergeant. They couldn't put NCOs in general population without their consent. I wasn't about to go to P.C., so I signed the consent form.

Ann visited me every Sunday, and my attorneys kept me abreast of what was going on with my case. I found out that my trial had been rigged from the beginning. The entire jury was under the command of Colonel Anderson, the division commander who wanted me to be found guilty and out of the Marines. Don't get me wrong. I was guilty on all counts. I had done everything they said I did, and more, but my point is, I never had a chance at a fair trial. The jury was under "unofficial orders" to find me guilty.

Prisoners that didn't have regular job assignments were sometimes sent out on details, picking up trash on the side of the roads. I was assigned to one of those details one day when I got the shock of my life. I was walking to the truck that I was supposed to ride on, when I saw one of the guards staring at me, with a big smile on his face. It was Williams' friend, the one I had ripped off and started to shoot when he was in my house that day. He walked up to me and said, "You ain't so tough now, are you? Get on the truck." I didn't know that he was a prison guard. Now I was supposed to walk down a deserted road with him? I don't think so.

I knew that if I got on that truck, he was going to kill me and say that I had tried to escape. So I grabbed my chest and fell to the ground, faking a heart attack. They took me to sick bay, and I was put on bed rest for a few days. After that, I was assigned to work in the library.

I had one agenda. That was, to get off of "The Hill" and into minimum custody where I would have some freedom. I stayed out of trouble, worked hard, and did everything they told me. It paid off. I made minimum in less than a month.

Minimum security was in 24 Area, and it was one big party. I volunteered to work in the mess hall because we worked side by side with people who were not in confinement, and it was open to everyone. Therefore, we had all of the drugs and alcohol we wanted.

Williams came by and brought me some weed from time to time. He also brought me some bad news. My mother's friend in Los Angeles refused to pay him the money that he owed us. I told him not to do anything until I got out. I wanted to kick his butt personally. Although I was incarcerated, I still needed my money. Williams was paying my car note and some of my other expenses with my part of our drug proceeds, but they were trying to build a case against him too, so I didn't know how long that would work.

Ann was still visiting me every week. However, with my being in minimum security, I was able to sneak out and walk down the road where she would sit waiting in her car and we had a little private time together.

I found out that "Earth Wind & Fire" was going to be in Los Angeles. I last saw them when they were in San Diego, just before I was locked up. I thought they were the best group ever. They really put on a good show. I started to work on a plan to see them.

On the night of the concert, I was going to sneak out after count and have Ann pick me up with a change of clothes. We were going to go to the concert, and then I was going to sneak back in. After thinking about it, I realized how dumb that idea really was. If I had gotten caught, there is no way they would believe that I was just going to see Earth, Wind, & Fire, and was coming back after the concert. Besides, escape carried a mandatory two-year sentence, and I was only doing six months total now.

One day, my attorney came to see me with good news. Colonel Anderson had had a heart attack and was in the hospital. He said the acting commander had agreed to reduce my jail time, and I would be home for Thanksgiving. That never happened. Colonel Anderson blocked it from his hospital bed. A few days later I found out they were going to send me to Leavenworth to do the rest of my time. Nobody wanted to go there.

Williams' case was coming up soon, so I asked him to put me on his witness list. I figured that would keep me at the brig for a while. I was wrong. They dropped the charges on Williams, and on the day before Thanksgiving, I was on a plane headed to Leavenworth Federal Penitentiary. During the plane ride, I was trying to figure out what I had done to piss those people off so badly. Why would they send me to a federal prison for five months?

During the plane ride, we had to make an emergency stop in Amarillo, Texas. I don't know what the problem was, but it took them a couple of hours to fix it. While we were sitting there, I was reflecting on my life up until that point. I thought about my first church, the Rose of Sharon Missionary Baptist Church, and how I loved to hear Rev. Murphy preach. I thought about how happy I

CHAPTER 5 - The Hoodlum

was when I was baptized, and how proud I was as I stood my post as a junior usher.

I thought about the night that I preached my trial sermon, and all the fun I had with Dub, Kennedy, and all of my friends at the St. James COGIC. And here I was, sitting on a plane that was headed to one of the most notorious prisons in the country, Leavenworth.

How had I messed my life up so badly? At that point, I didn't care if the plane crashed and shattered into a million pieces. Much like my dreams had, but there was no such luck. The plane was repaired and some time that night I arrived at, "The United States Disciplinary Barracks" in Leavenworth, Kansas.

The first place that we were taken was "Processing." There, we were evaluated, and given uniforms, job assignments, and inmate numbers. Mine was *59698*. I told them that my hobby was playing the flute, so they asked if I wanted to audition for the prison band. I told them that I would. They set it up for later that week. We were taken to a segregated area, and we all went to sleep.

When I woke up the next morning, I looked around trying to figure out where I was. Then it dawned on me and a sick feeling came over me. As if that wasn't bad enough, I remembered what day it was, Thanksgiving. I remember asking myself, "What do I have to be thankful for?" My attorney told me a couple of weeks earlier, "You'll be home for Thanksgiving."

After about a week, we were taken to general population. Each wing had eight tiers (floors). Everything was made of either iron, steel, or concrete. They were all one-man cells, which was fine with me. Up until that point, I had lived in open dorms.

A few days later, I was called to the band room for my audition. I really didn't think I was going to get in because I couldn't read music, which was one of the requirements. I had been taking flute lessons and had just started learning to read when I was arrested.

When I got to the band room, I was about to go in when I saw someone walking down the hall towards me, (I later found out that his name was Driver and he was doing a double life sentence for two murders.) When he got closer, he said, "Well, well, what do we have here? Is it a he or a she?" In prison you don't answer a question like that with words. You answer it with your fist. I went after him, but before we could start fighting, the sergeant came out and broke things up.

The band director was on sick leave, and the sergeant was filling in for him while he was out. He didn't know a lot about music and was there mostly for security purposes.

There were rooms where the different sections practiced before the whole band came together. There were no flutes in the band room, and I was waiting to get mine from home, so I started off playing (or trying to play) the alto saxophone. The fingering on the sax is close to the fingering on the flute, so I was able to play well enough to fool the sergeant into letting me join the band.

There was one other flutist there. His name was Rogers, and he was doing triple life for three murders. Rogers was a short, quiet young man that stayed to himself. Most of the time he didn't practice with anyone else. He just stood in the hallway facing one of the corners and played all by himself, and boy, could he play.

I learned a lot from Rogers. The most important thing I learned was never to say I "blew" the flute, and not to let anyone else say it either. He told me to always say that I "play" the flute. In prison, using the wrong phrase can get you into a lot of trouble.

One day, I was in one of the breakout rooms by myself, playing "Georgia on my mind" when Driver walked in and sat down with two other dudes, Bullock and Livingston. I thought they were coming at me because of the confrontation that Driver and I had a couple of weeks earlier. I asked them what was going on. Livingston told me to keep playing. When I finished playing, Livingston told me that they had a jazz combo that played separate from the band. He asked me if I wanted to play with them. After that, I was in the jazz combo.

Livingston was the leader of the group. He was a thin, light skinned brother with long, wild looking hair. He was one of the baddest dudes on keyboards that I had ever heard. He reminded me of Herbie Hancock. Driver played alto and tenor sax. He looked like Grover Washington Jr., and he played like him too. Bullock played bass like he was born with it in his hands. There was one other person in the combo, a very talented drummer named Curtis.

116

CHAPTER 5 - The Hoodlum

When I first heard them play, I was scared to death. These brothers sounded as good as any group I'd ever heard. Most of them had played professionally before they came to prison. Why did they want me to play with them? I wasn't in their caliber. I later found out that Rogers was going through some personal problems and no longer wanted to play. So he recommended me.

Experience wasn't the only difference between the rest of the combo and me. They were all convicted murderers, serving life sentences or more. I was a drug dealer and con man, serving six months. I loved playing with those guys, I learned a lot, but it wasn't easy. Livingston pushed me harder than my music teacher ever had. I played some notes on the flute that I didn't even know were there.

Everyone in the prison had a job. Mine was playing in the band. I was in the band area eight hours a day, five days a week. In the evenings and on weekends, I was in the cellblock watching television or in my cell reading or listening to jazz on the prison radio network.

The band director had been out for so long, I was starting to think he wasn't coming back. I was glad of that because I still couldn't read music. With the help of some of the brothers in the band, I was able to fool the sergeant, but everyone knew that I wouldn't be able to fool the director for very long. So they were trying to teach me what they could before he returned.

When I got to the band area one Monday morning, we were called to the band room. I felt my heart sink when I found out that the director was back and had called a special practice for everyone. He handed out some sheet music and gave us the tempo. I had no idea what was on that sheet, but I put it on the stand in front of me and started playing along with everyone else.

After a few minutes he stopped us and said that something was wrong. He had each section to play separately. When he got to my section, I looked at the music sheet like I was reading, and started playing along with everyone. After about a minute, he stopped us. He pointed to me and asked me who I was. After I told him, he said, "You can't read, can you?" I said, "Yes, I can read." He walked over and took the music sheet off of my stand and put a different one on it. Then he said, "Play that." I looked

117

down at the music sheet and just started playing something. He looked at me and yelled, "You can't read music." I looked at him and said, "Oh. You meant music." Just as I was afraid of, I was kicked out of the band, but because of Livingston, Driver, and the others, he let me stay in the Jazz combo.

One day, I was called down to my counselor's office. He said that I had an emergency phone call. When I picked up the phone, it was dad. God had dropped a dime on me again. Dad told me that God had let him know that I was in trouble and needed him. He said that he had gotten permission from the warden to visit me that weekend. He said that he would be there on Friday.

Dad and I had a good time visiting. He rode the Greyhound from Chicago and stayed at a hotel in town. He came to the prison to see me on Friday and Saturday. The chaplain asked him to come back on Sunday for morning worship and to preach at the chapel. I was so proud of him. The brothers at the chapel asked me to come back and worship with them. I told them that I would, but I never did. Dad went home after church on Sunday. During the rest of my time there, we kept in touch.

Other than the brothers that were in the band, I didn't associate with a lot of people while I was in prison. Mostly, I kept to myself and read. One of the books I read was, "The Autobiography of Malcolm X." That book really made me think.

Sometimes I would hang out with some of the brothers that I was in the brig with at Camp Pendleton. We would go to the movies on the weekends or play basketball or cards. One Sunday, I was on my way to the movie theater, but I changed my mind because I wanted to hear the jazz program on the radio. I was glad that I didn't go because there was a riot in the theater. It was not like the riot at the brig. The guards put a stop to it right away. Then they sent the "Goon Squad" to the cell of everyone that was at the theater to beat them up. There was yelling and screaming all night long.

I learned something else while I was there, don't mess with children or old people. There was a dude on our cellblock that was convicted of raping a five-year-old-girl. We enjoyed making his life miserable. We constantly beat, kicked, and stomped him. He stayed in his cell and refused to come out. One night, everyone on the cellblock took turns urinating in a bucket, then someone threw it on him. They finally took him to P.C. (Protective Custody).

There was a big talent show coming up, and we were going to play in it. We decided to play the hit song, "The Hustle." That was going to be the first song that we played where the flute was the lead. In all of the other songs, I just played bits and pieces.

We practiced a few times and things went really well. A few days before the show, I got some good news. I was getting out a month early. So, in March of 1976, the day before I was supposed to play in the big show, I walked out of Leavenworth, a free man. Although I was no longer in prison, I was not truly free.

I once read that when a flea trainer is training his fleas, he places them in a jar. At first, they jump out because fleas are incredible jumpers. But the training begins when he puts the lid on the jar. The fleas continue to jump, but now they bump their heads on the lid over and over again. After a while, the fleas continue to jump, but they no longer jump high enough to bump their heads. When the trainer removes the lid, the fleas continue to jump, but they won't jump out of the jar. Actually, they won't jump out because they no longer can jump out. They have conditioned themselves to jump only so high. Now, they think that is all that they can do.

Too many of our young men and women have been conditioned to not jump high. It's as though Satan has placed a lid over their dreams. Every time they have tried to jump high, they bump their heads. Someone was always telling them what they could not do, or what they could not be. They've bumped their heads so many times, that now they think all they can do is sell drugs, run with the gangs, or hustle in the streets. But Jesus Christ is able to restore our dreams and give us hope. Too bad I didn't realize it at the time.

When I got to San Diego, my friends were there to welcome me home. We partied and got high most of the night. When the smoke cleared, I found out that some things had changed while I was gone. First of all, Williams wasn't able to keep up my car payments because business was down and he had trouble collecting some of our money.

Also, one of Ann's old friends had gotten out of prison, and they had been spending time together. I don't know if they had been sexually involved or not, but when I asked her what was going on, she told me not to ask her about anything that happened while I was in prison, so I didn't.

Williams and I were able to collect some of the money that people owed us, including my mother's old friend, but we weren't able to get back to "business as usual." I decided it was time to take a trip to Chicago. It had been a long time since I had been there. Since I was going, I decided to take a few kilos of weed with me, but there was a drought going on, and no one could find any anywhere.

There was a Mexican brother, Natchez, that was living upstairs. He had a lot of connections, so I was able to get half an ounce of high quality cocaine from him. I didn't have all of the money, so I worked out a deal where I would pay him the rest when I got back. I told Ann that I would be back in two weeks, but she had a feeling that wouldn't happen. For the last day or two before I left, she just moped around the house and played the record "Misty Blue" over and over again.

It felt good to be home even though a lot of things had changed. Mother and Dad, although they still lived in the same house, had moved into separate bedrooms. Dad took me and Ralph's old room. Ralph and Deborah's children, Nooky (Valisha) and Dewayne, were school age, and Rose and Troy had bought a new house on 117th and Throop.

One of the first things I did when I got to Chicago, what I always do when I go there, went to Dave's. There are some foods that I look forward to eating whenever I go to Chicago. Dave's Polish is one of them. Others are: Jew Town polishes, Italian beef sandwiches, Italian lemonade, and Italian Ice.

I was glad to be home again and spend time with my family and friends. Jeri was in Chicago too, so I thought it was a good time for us to talk. I wasn't buying that story about "us" having a baby. The last time we had sex, or had even seen each other was after I had gotten out of boot camp, the first week of March in 1972. The baby was born on February 13, 1973, more than eleven months later.

I didn't want to talk to Jeri to confront her or accuse her of anything. On the contrary, I was still in love with her, and I wanted her to know that whatever happened while we were separated didn't matter. We weren't together then, and we didn't know if we would ever be together again. Besides, I had slept with a lot of women during that time. The difference was I couldn't get pregnant, but I could have gotten someone else pregnant.

I borrowed Ralph's car and took Jeri to Douglas Park so we could talk. I told her how I felt about everything and how I hoped we could be a family again. I told her that I didn't care if the baby wasn't mine. She'd had Everett before we'd met, and I loved him. But she tried to convince me that the baby was mine. I felt like I was being insulted, and I became angry and hurt. I decided that the best thing for us would be to go our separate ways.

Dad kept trying to get me back in church, but I was too busy partying and having fun. I stayed at Ralph's crib, but I spent a lot of time on the south side at Rose's. I wasn't there for vacation only. I had business to take care of. The drug business.

The cocaine went faster than I thought it would. Ralph hooked me up with C.J. and Red. They had both grown up in the neighborhood, and were in the pimp game. C.J. was one of Vivian's little brothers, and as you might remember, Red was the one that I had been arrested with before I went to the Marines. C.J. headed a group of pimps that hung out together on the north side. I started hanging out with them and some of the other players. I needed more cocaine. I had to make a trip back to San Diego.

When I got to San Diego, Ann was glad to see me but was disappointed when she found out that I wasn't staying long. I tried, unsuccessfully, to get some heroin on consignment from her friend. I wanted to make the same deal with him that I'd made with Natchez. So, I paid Natchez what I owed him and got another package of cocaine. This time I got an ounce. As before, I told him that I would pay him his share when I got back. But when I boarded the plane for Chicago, I had a feeling that I would not be going back. I had seen the last of Ann, Williams, and Andretti. San Diego and Natchez had seen the last of his drugs and his money.

I usually stayed at Ralph's, sleeping on his couch. I also had a room at Rose's house. Larraine, Rose's oldest daughter, let me use her room whenever I was there. Most of the time, though, I hung out with C.J., Red, and the other players.

C.J. hooked me up with Walt, who was part owner of a real nice nightclub on Madison Avenue called, "The Flip Side." Walt was looking for some cocaine that was un-cut. I tried to do business with him several times. Each time I went to him, I put less cut on the "product," but there were several different tests that he used. So every time I went to him I heard those same words, "Thanks, but no thanks."

All of the players were wearing perms (Super Fly hair styles) at the time, so I decided to get mine done too. One Saturday morning, C.J. and Red took me to a shop on Madison Avenue called Freddy's.

Freddy's was not your usual barbershop. There was drinking and drugging in the shop, so the door was always locked. If Freddy didn't know you, or you were not with someone that he knew, he would not let you in. Freddy was gay, but that was where all of the players and hustlers on the west side got their hair done. He was one of the best hairdressers around.

I carried my gun with me everywhere I went, including to church. I wanted to be ready if Natchez and his boys came at me. I didn't go to church very often. Actually, I think I only went once during this period. I thought God was angry with me for leaving the church and the ministry.

Ann and I talked every once in a while. I still cared for her, and in a sense, I wanted to go back to her, but I was too caught up in the fast life that I had gotten into in Chicago.

I decided to open a franchise similar to the one that Williams and I had in San Diego. This time the product would be cocaine instead of marijuana. I brought on Q, a brother that I had known from the hood, to work the business. Since everyone else was selling quarter ($25.00) bags of coke, I decided to sell dime (10.00) bags, for those who couldn't afford the $25.00.

I gave Q thirteen bags and told him that when he sold them, give me $100.00 and I would give him more bags, but he disappeared on me. I looked for him and left messages for two weeks. Finally, I tricked Emma, his girlfriend, into giving me his mother's phone number. I called her and told her that her son had something that belonged to me, and if she didn't want him to get hurt, he'd better get in touch with me very soon. About 20 minutes later the phone rang. It was Q. He told me that he didn't appreciate me calling his mother. I told him that I didn't appreciate him running off with my product. He said he had my money. So we arranged to meet at Mom's, a small tavern on Roosevelt, at 6:00 PM.

I felt uneasy about the upcoming meeting with Q. Maybe it was our phone conversation, maybe it was a sixth sense. Why had he dodged me for two weeks, and then, all of a sudden he wanted to meet up so he could pay me? No. Something was wrong. I could feel it.

Ralph had just gotten home from work, and he could tell something was wrong with me. I told him about my meeting with Q. He said that he was going with me. I couldn't let him do that. Ralph had a wife and two young children. Not only was he a family man but, he was one of the community's leaders. He had, in my opinion, the perfect life. The kind of life that I had always secretly wanted. It was too late for me; I had made too many bad choices. I had to accept who and what I had become. I was a hoodlum.

I told Ralph that I would be OK, he didn't have to go with me. He insisted by saying that he was my brother and that he had to be sure that nothing was going to happen to me. Then he told me to let him know when I was ready to go. I knew I couldn't let Ralph go with me. It was too dangerous. I went into his room and told him that I had changed my mind and wasn't going. I told him that I was going to the store to get some beer and would be right back. I stepped into the hallway and checked my pistol to make sure it was fully loaded. Then I walked around the corner to Mom's and waited for Q.

I got there a few minutes early to check out the surroundings in case I was being set up. I went inside and looked around, then, I went outside and waited. I wanted to see Q, and who was with him, before he got there. A few minutes after six a car pulled up, but it wasn't Q. It was the Slick Boys. Another car pulled up on the other side of the street. When they got out of their cars, one of them pointed at me and said, "There he is." Q had set me up.

THE HOODLUM PREACHER

I turned and started walking into the tavern. One of the officers shouted, "Halt." I got in the tavern and closed the door behind me. I always carried my gun in a clip on holster, and wore it on my belt behind my back. When I got in the tavern, I snatched the holster and gun off and threw it behind the bar. Then I stood there like I was trying to order a drink. A few seconds later, I felt the cold steel of the barrel of a pistol pressed against the side of my neck.

The officer told me that I had done a stupid thing by not stopping when told. He said that he came very close to shooting me because they were told that I was armed and dangerous. I was arrested and taken to jail. For the second time in my life I was charged with unlawful use of a weapon. My bond was $100.00. I called Ralph and he posted my bond and got me out. When I went to court, I signed the bond money over to a lawyer. He got the case dismissed.

I was running out of work (cocaine), but I couldn't go back to California. I had gotten the word that Natchez had put a hit out on me. When I talked to Ann, I also found out that she was pregnant. I wondered if the baby was mine or her "friend's." I also wondered if she was really pregnant, or was she just trying to get me to go back to San Diego. In any event, I couldn't go back, at least not then.

Walt called to let me know that he had gotten a large quantity of high quality cocaine. As a matter of fact, the cocaine that Walt had was better than what I was getting from California. I started getting ounces from him and paying him after they were sold.

One evening, a dude from the neighborhood, Mickey, came by Ralph's to get some cocaine. He had a beautiful young lady with him, named Esther. Her nickname was Pete. When the Commodores made the record, "Brick House," they had her in mind. When I found out that she and Mickey were just friends, we started dating. About a week later, I moved in with her. She had a small, two-bedroom apartment on Madison that she shared with her four-year old daughter. Besides cocaine, we also snorted a lot of uncut heroin, called "P" for pure.

I learned that Walt was looking for a new partner for his nightclub. Clark, his current partner, wanted to get out of the business. Walt told me that I could buy half of the club for $28,500. I talked to a couple of people that I thought might be able to come up with the money. That didn't work, so I came up with the dumbest plan imaginable.

Clark knew some people that made loans. Against his advice, I had him arrange a loan for me for $20,000. The interest rate was 50% per week. I figured I could buy a large quantity of heroin and cocaine and more than triple my money. That way, I would be able to pay back the loan and have the money for the club.

Oh. I forgot to mention something. I had a habit of messing up whenever I got my hands on a lot of drugs or money.

Clark told me to meet him at the meeting place one Thursday night at 9:00 pm. He was going to take me to the loan sharks. I went to The Flip Side, where we'd always met, and waited for him. He never showed up, so after about two hours, I left. When I talked to him the next day, he asked me what happened to me. I found out that when he told me to meet him at the meeting place, he wasn't talking about the place where we usually met. He was talking about a nightclub called, "The Meeting Place." I also found out that the sharks had changed their mind about loaning me the money, thank God. So I gave up on the idea of buying the club

Clark had some heroin that he was trying to sell. I convinced him to give it to me to sell for him. A couple of days later, Clark was found in the trunk of his car with five bullets in him. Since he wasn't going to need his money, I kept it.

It was during that time that I started Fuzzy on heroin. As a matter of fact, I was the one who first stuck a needle in his arm just like Tadpole had done to me eight years earlier.

I went to Fuzzy's one Sunday afternoon. Some of his friends were there and they were drinking and shooting some Tee's and Blues, the poor man's heroin. I had never heard of them before, but when they asked me if I wanted some, I said yes. Fuzzy shot the drugs into my arm, but it must have been too much for the first time because I O.D.'d and passed out. When I came to, I was lying on the kitchen floor.

Later that evening, when the drugs started wearing off, my shoulder was really hurting. Dad went with me to Cook County Hospital, where I learned that my shoulder was disconnected. My arm was in a sling for a few days, but it was still business as usual.

I was at Freddy's on Saturday, waiting to get my hair done. One of the more successful pimps was sitting in one of the chairs. While he was getting his hair done, he was sharing his philosophy of life with the other patrons.

He said, "You know, there are two kinds of people in this world, the players and the squares. The squares have to get up and go to work every day, because that's the only way they can make any money. They don't know how to play the game.

But us players, we know the game. We drive the baddest rides. We got the prettiest women. We got all the money. We do whatever we want to do, whenever we want to do it." Then he said, "I don't know about y'all, but as long as I live, I'm gonna be a player."

I talked to C.J. about the pimp game. He schooled me on how the game was played. C.J. was a real Mack. Not one of those, "Popsicle Pimps." I tried to talk Esther into hooking up with some of C.J.s women, but she wasn't hearing that. She offered to get a job and give me the money but I knew that wouldn't be enough. So, I came up with another scheme.

About a week before Christmas, I opened a savings account at a small bank on 26th Street. I gave them $2000.00 in cash and wrote a check from Ann and my old account in San Diego for $4000.00. I told them that I had just gotten out of the Marines and had moved to Chicago. I was transferring the money from my account in California and opening an account there. I knew that it would take about 10 days before they found out that my check was no good, so I had to work fast.

After a couple of days, I withdrew $1500.00. I knew there would be no problem with that because I had given them more than that in cash. I went back on Christmas Eve and withdrew another $1000.00. A few days later, I went back and made another withdrawal of $1000.00. I had almost walked out without the money because the teller was in the back room for so long.

I figured that it was time to leave the bank alone. I had made $1500.00 off of them, and they would soon find out that I had given them a bogus check. On the night before New Year's Eve, I received a call from Mother, who was visiting our relatives in St. Louis. She told me that all of her money had been stolen. She asked me if I could send her some. Against my better judgment, I decided to hit the bank one more time.

It was the morning of New Year's Eve, so the bank was crowded. I filled out a withdrawal slip for $500.00 and got in line. When I gave the teller my bankbook and slip, she disappeared into the back. It seemed like she was back there forever. I started to walk out, but I remembered what had happened the last time, so I waited. After a few minutes, I decided it was time to go, but it was too late.

Before I could turn around, I felt someone grab my arms from behind and handcuffs were placed on my wrists. They took me to a room and started questioning me. I showed them my military I.D. and told them that I had recently gotten discharged, and I was a Vietnam veteran. I told them that Ann must have closed our account because she was mad at me. Then, I told them that I wanted to press charges against her for stealing my money. The president of the bank was in the room at the time and agreed to drop the charges when I got to court if I paid back the money.

I spent New Year's Eve in jail. The next day, Dad and Ralph came and got me. A few weeks later, I got a message from Clark's girlfriend. I was glad to hear from her because she was very pretty, and with Clark out of the way, I wanted her for myself. When I called her, she said, "Clark wants his money." I was so shocked, all I could say was, "I thought he was dead."

It turned out that Clark had survived the shooting. He was in intensive care and wanted his girlfriend to get the money that I owed him. I didn't have it. I'd used it to finance the con that I had run on the bank.

I came up with the money to pay the bank, but by the time I went to court, I'd spent it. After the second time, the judge told me that if I came back again without the money, bring my toothbrush because I was going to jail.

One Sunday, my nephew, Christopher, who everyone called Christaball, and my cousin, Jug, drove my mother back to Chicago from St. Louis. I was due in court on the next day, but I still didn't have the bank's money. I decided to ride back to St. Louis with them and lay low there for a while.

On our way to the highway, we went to Esther's to get my clothes. She had come into some money and bought a nice supply of heroin. When I saw that she wasn't home, I decided to take the heroin that she had in the house. I figured I could sell it in St. Louis and have some money to live off of for a few days.

St. Louis was as different as night and day from Chicago; St. Louis had no nightlife. I got a very disturbing call from Ralph. Esther was telling people that I had molested her daughter. I knew why she was doing it. She was angry because I had stolen her drugs and left but I didn't appreciate her spreading that lie. Not only would I never mess with a child, but I also know what happens to child molesters in prison.

One thing that I really liked about St. Louis was the family get-togethers at my cousin Nita's house. Every Sunday she would cook a big meal, and all of the family and friends would get together to eat, drink, and play bid whist.

During the first week or two, I stayed in my grandmother's apartment in the Vaughn Projects. My sister, Shirley, my two nieces, Christine and Sharon (Dee Dee), and Christine's husband, Jesse, lived there too. Shirley was the oldest of my siblings. She was born during my mother's first marriage and was raised in St. Louis by my grandmother. Christine, Christopher (aka Chris or Christaball), and Dee Dee were her children. My grandmother raised them also.

Chris was living in St. Louis County with his girlfriend, Faye. The make-up of the St. Louis area is hard to describe. It is divided into two main jurisdictions, St. Louis City and St. Louis County.

I met a cousin that I didn't know I had. His name was Bobby, and his wife's name was Irene. They had a house on Goodfellow and we all got to be very close. Bobby and I became drinking buddies, and Irene was my hairdresser. She worked part time at a cleaning company and was able to get me hired there too, working from 6 pm till midnight. For the first time in six years, I had a job.

I decided to try to play it straight. I was going to leave the fast life alone and be a square, but I was not going to stop smoking weed. I moved in with Chris and Faye and lived in their basement. That worked out good for me because they lived around the corner from Bobby and Irene, and I rode to work with her.

The job only lasted a couple of months. My supervisor started riding my back, trying to make me quit so she could hire her nephew. It worked, but not the way she expected. She finally got on my last nerve, I cornered her in her office, cursed her out, and threatened to kick her behind. After Irene calmed me down, security escorted me out of the building. Not only was I kicked out of the building, I couldn't even wait in Irene's car because they made me leave the parking lot.

I got a job working at the Woolworth store at River Roads Mall. I was not an employee of the Woolworth Company, or in the management-training program. I just worked at that store; it felt good to be back on the floor again. I met a young lady who worked at the lunch counter named Myra. We started dating and spending a lot of time together. I got home one night after a date with her and found a beautiful woman sleeping in my bed. She said her name was Deborah and she was a friend of Faye's. She also said that Faye didn't think I would mind sharing my bed with her. She was right. I didn't mind at all.

I started dating Myra and Deborah. Myra was very dark skinned. Deborah was white. She moved in with me in Faye's basement and we had a very good relationship.

One Saturday night, Nita's social club, The Gaylarks, had their annual dance. It was a big event because The Gaylarks were well known in the club circle. By the way, they had nothing to do with homosexuality. They had been around since the 50s or 60s. At that time "gay" meant "happy."

I showed up at the dance, fashionably late, dressed in a white suit with Myra on one arm and Deborah on the other. I had the attention of almost everybody in the dance hall. After that, I had the reputation of being a player.

Although I liked Deborah, I was uncomfortable with some of the looks that I was getting from some of the "sisters." So we eventually broke up. I broke up with Myra too. She was sweating me too much, wanting a committed relationship. I wasn't ready for that.

Nita worked at a medical center on Grand Boulevard. She always stopped at a club close by after work to unwind before going home. Sometimes I would meet her there. One Friday evening, we were sitting at the bar when I saw the finest woman in the world walk in and sit down. I went over to her table and asked her to dance. Afterwards, I bought her a drink and we talked for a while. Her name was Gwen. She was tall and light-skinned with long, brown hair. She had a beautiful smile and the prettiest eyes I had ever seen.

We started dating, and a few weeks later I moved in with her. She had a cute little daughter, Nikki, and an infant son, Tony. She worked as personnel manager of Six Flags Over St. Louis. Before long, we rented a pretty little house on Blackstone, next door to my Uncle Johnny.

Although Gwen and I had some problems, we were very happy together. We loved each other and wanted to get married. The problem was that we both had to get divorces from our current spouses first.

I got a call from Mother telling me that Chucky was dead. He'd had a massive heart attack. Chucky was one of my oldest and dearest friends. I'd known him as long as I could remember. I'd had other friends that had died, but Chucky was the first one that had grown up with me. He was only 30 years old.

I wanted to make the relationship between Gwen and me work, but I didn't have my priorities straight. I still had a lot of party in me. She wanted us to spend quality time together at home. I wanted to hang out with the fellows, drink beer, and smoke weed.

I was working in the sporting goods department selling rifles during hunting season. I had increased their business by almost 50%, but they wouldn't increase my salary or give me a bonus. One day, I decided that Woolworth should share some of the money that I was making for them. So I kept some of it. They got mad and fired me.

I got a job as assistant manager of Noble Shoe Store in Jamestown Mall. It was different than anything that I had done, but I liked it. That was about the time that I found out that Jane Byrne had been elected mayor of Chicago. I hated that woman so much; I vowed not to return to Chicago as long as she was mayor. Not even to visit. One day, I got a call from Mother saying that dad was very sick. He was in the hospital and asking for me. I got to Chicago the next day and went straight to the hospital. As I was walking into Dad's room, I heard him ask someone, "Did Burt get here yet?"

I found out that Dad had appendicitis. They caught everything in time and he would be fine. While I was in Chicago, I wouldn't drive at all because I was wanted, and I didn't want to be stopped by the police. I was glad to be able to spend time with dad at the hospital and with my daughter, Andi.

I couldn't wait to get back home to Gwen. She had started her divorce process and we were anticipating spending the rest of our lives together. I hadn't done anything to start on mine. I wanted to get the divorce, but I didn't want to spend the money to do it. I had more important things to do with my money, like buying reefer and beer.

I had fallen behind in my car payments. I woke up one morning and found out it had been repossessed. I needed about $1200.00 to get it back and I didn't have it. I had to get the car back because my niece, Christine, had co-signed for me and I didn't want to mess up her credit. I staged a break-in at the store and took the bank deposit. They gave me a polygraph (lie detector test) to see if I'd had anything to do with the theft. I passed with flying colors.

I got my car back, but since paying bills was not high on my list of priorities, a few months later it was repossessed again. I thank God that they resold it for more than I owed so Christine's credit wasn't affected.

I started riding the bus to and from work. One day I was standing at the bus stop when a brother that worked in one of the stores in the mall stopped and picked me up. His name was

131

THE HOODLUM PREACHER

Charlie, and he lived not too far from me. We became good friends and started hanging out at a jazz club, "The Moose", sometimes after work. They had live shows there every night featuring a group called, "The Bozeman Twins."

After about eight months at the shoe store, I was promoted to manager, that didn't last long. Before I was promoted, I had been writing phony refunds and selling shoes under the table. One Saturday morning, I was cooking breakfast and Gwen was sitting in the living room talking with our insurance agent, when the doorbell rang. When she opened the door, there were two detectives standing there. They arrested me and took me to the St. Louis County Jail in Clayton. I was released later that day.

The following Monday, I started working at Radio Shack in Jamestown Mall. Charlie hooked me up with a friend of his that had a car to sell. It was a hoopty, but it beat walking and catching the bus.

Every time we got a new gadget at the store, I brought it home and Gwen and I played with it or tried it out. One day, we got some telephone bugging devices. I took one home that night to show it to Gwen, but she wasn't home. I plugged it up to the phone that was on the bar and started calling people. I had fun taping them, but I was pretty high so I went to bed.

The next morning, Gwen went to work before I got up. I had forgotten about the bugging device, so I left if on the bar when I went to work. It was the kind of bugging device that started when the phone receiver was picked up and stopped when it was hung up. I couldn't wait to get home so Gwen and I could listen to the tape I'd made the night before but she wasn't home again.

I opened a can of beer, lit a joint, and started playing the tape. After a while, I realized that I had recorded some of Gwen's phone calls from earlier that evening. There were calls to or from her grandmother or her friend, Carolyn. I really didn't want to listen to her dull, private conversations, so I walked to the stereo to turn off the tape and put on a record.

Just as I reached for the "stop" button, I heard a man's voice say, "Is it cool?" I stopped in my tracks. He said it again, "Is it cool?" Then I heard Gwen's voice say, "Yeah. It's cool. He never gets home from work until after ten." I heard her telling him how much she had enjoyed herself the night before, and later, telling Carolyn that that was the first time she had cheated. I was devastated. I was in a state of shock. I didn't know what else to do, so I went to bed.

Gwen didn't come home at all that night. She got in the next morning just in time to change clothes and go to work. She tried to start an argument with me. I guess the best defense is a good offense. I didn't even argue back. I just asked, "Who is Charles?" Her mouth flew open and her eyes got big. She said, "What?" I said it again, "Who is Charles?" She asked me how I knew about him. I asked her what they were doing the last two nights. I could tell that she was trying to figure out how I had found out. She started apologizing and saying she had made a mistake. She asked me to forgive her and said she would never do it again. Then she went to work.

I wanted to believe her because I loved her so much. All of that time, the bugging device had been sitting on top of the bar in plain view, but she never saw it. I took it down to the basement, plugged it into a jack, and hid it in the ceiling. When I got home that night Gwen was there. We talked for a while and I thought everything was all right.

I told her that I was going downstairs to watch the rest of the ball game. When I got there, I pulled out the tape. I was hoping to hear her tell Charles that I knew what was going on and it was over. Instead, she told him that I knew what was going on, and they had to be more careful.

After that, I had a new hobby. Every night when I got home, I went to the basement and listened to her and Charles' conversations. I let her know that I knew what was going on. They never found out how I knew. They thought I was having them followed. Eventually we broke up and she started packing her things to move out.

I was working on commission at Radio Shack, so the more merchandise I sold, the more money I made. Steve, the manager, was gone a lot, so I was often stuck in the back office doing reports and other paperwork. Therefore, I wasn't making a lot of money. So, I decided to rip off the bank deposit to make up for my loss.

133

They gave everyone a polygraph test in an effort to find the thief. I passed the test just like I had done at Noble Shoes. Jeff, a part time salesman, failed. He said that he was nervous at the time. I felt sorry for Jeff. He was a grammar school teacher with a family, working a part time job, trying to make ends meet, but then again, he might have failed the test because he was stealing too, and was not as good a liar as I was. I hate that he lost his job. I liked Jeff.

One evening after I had gotten off work, I was sitting in the parking lot in my car rolling a joint when the police pulled up. I stuck the weed in my shoe and stepped out of the car. They didn't find the weed, but there was a warrant out for my arrest pertaining to the bogus refunds at Noble Shoes. They took me to the jail in Florissant and held me there until the county picked me up.

Before they put me in the cell they made me take off my shoes and belt. I still had the weed in my left shoe, under the insole. When they put me in the cell, I kept watching my shoes to see if they were going to search them. After about an hour, I lay on the bench and went to sleep. Some time later, they woke me up and told me that the county was there to get me.

When I was putting my shoes on, they stopped me. One of the officers told me to turn them over and shake them. I figured they had searched them while I was sleeping and found the weed, but I had to play it out. I shook the right shoe and put it on. Then I picked up the left shoe and shook it very lightly. The weed fell out. I told them that that was not my weed, and it wasn't in my shoe when they locked me up. One of them told me that I had a choice. I could either eat the reefer, or be charged with it. I ate it.

Mother was visiting St. Louis at the time, so she convinced her brother, Uncle Archie, to put up his house as property bond for me. I was released the next day, but as soon as they finished processing me out, I was arrested by a police officer from another municipality on some other charge.

When I got to the other station, mother and Gwen were waiting there to bond me out and take me home. Mother told me how nice and helpful Gwen had been to her, and how lucky I was to have her. What she didn't know was most of her things had already been moved out of the house, and she was moving the next day.

When we got home, I wanted so much to beg her to stay and give it another try. But my pride wouldn't let me. I couldn't show any sign of weakness or vulnerability. I couldn't let her know that I still loved her. She moved to Dallas, and a few months later, she was married to someone she met there.

One Saturday I got a call from Bob, Radio Shack's district manager. I was being promoted to manager of the Bridgeton store. I called Gwen (not my ex-girlfriend) and told her of my promotion. Radio Shack had 28 stores in the St. Louis area, and only one black manager, Gwen. When I started working for them, Rodney was the only black manager, and Gwen was the only black trainee. Rodney managed the University City store. A few weeks later, on a Saturday, Gwen called to tell me that she had been promoted to manager of the Bayless store. A couple of hours later, Rodney called and told me that he had been fired. That made Gwen the only black manager and me the only black trainee. About an hour or so after I got to the Bridgeton store. I got a call from Gwen. She had been fired. I was starting to see a pattern.

It was about that time that my grandmother (Vassie Beck) died. She was my mother's mother, and my last grandparent. Her husband and my father's parents had all died in the 60s. She was a very strong Christian woman and I loved her very much.

Ralph and Deborah were having marital problems, so he came to St. Louis and moved in with me. A few weeks later, mother retired from her job. She came to St. Louis and moved in with me too. It was good for her because she was living next door to her sister.

I was at work one day when I got a call from a lady, asking to speak with the store manager. When I told her that I was the manager, she said that she had a complaint. She said that she was in my store a few days ago and a "nigger" waited on her. I knew it had to be me because I was the only black person at that store. I asked her was he rude or anything. She said, "No. He was very nice. I just don't like niggers waiting on me." She said that she would be in the store the next day and asked if I would be there. When I said I would, she asked if I would keep "that nigger" away from her and wait on her myself. I told her that I would be glad to. I told her that when she got to the store, ask for the manager.

I told my assistant, Steve, what had happened, and we devised a plan for the next day. The woman said that she would be in at about noon, so at 11:30 I went in my office and started doing paperwork and Steve worked the sales floor. Before long, Steve came to my office and said, "Burt, She's here." I slipped on my jacket and went out to meet her. I walked up to her, extended my hand, smiled, and said, "Hi. I'm Burton Barr, the store manager. We talked yesterday." Her eyes got big and her mouth fell open. She turned around and stormed out of the store.

On the Saturday after Christmas, William, the latest black trainee called to tell me that he had been promoted to store manager. After I congratulated him, I went to my office and started packing. Then I sat there and waited for Bob. He got there about an hour later. He said that things weren't working out and he was letting me go. He asked if I wanted to leave right away, or if I wanted to stay and help with inventory.

Anytime a store changes management, an inventory or audit has to be done to determine what the new manager is responsible for. I decided to stay, but not for the reasons they thought. Since the inventory wasn't done, technically, I was still the manager. So I wrote several phony refunds. After I had about two thousand dollars in my pocket, I told them I had changed my mind, and I left.

I decided to live off my unemployment checks for a while. I just got high and partied all of the time. I started dating Johnnie Mae, one of Irene's cousins and started shooting Tee's and Blues with my cousin, Tyrus. One day, I was shooting up in my basement and I OD'd just like I did at Fuzzy's a few years earlier. I dislocated my shoulder again, so my friend, J.R., took me to the hospital.

A few days later, dad called me and said that God had told him that I'd shot another overdose, just like I'd done in Chicago. I started wondering why God kept dropping dimes on me to dad every time I did something stupid.

I got tired of being at home, so I got a job at J.C. Penney's at River Roads Mall. On my third day there, they told me that I was going to be running the electronics department by myself the next morning until someone got there at noon. I was excited about that because I wanted to show them what I could do.

When I got off from work that night the police stopped me while I was walking to the bus stop. They told me that I fit the description of someone they were looking for. When they checked my I.D. they found out that I was wanted for failure to pay two traffic tickets. They placed me under arrest and took me to the Jennings police station.

When I went to court the next morning I pled guilty, thinking I would just get a fine and would still be able to get to work on time but the judge sentenced me to five days in the workhouse on each charge. After the judge said, "five days in the workhouse," I was waiting for him to say, "or else" so I would know how much my fine was. Instead, he said, "Next case." I said, "Wait a minute, Your Honor. You forgot to say, or else." The bailiff grabbed my arm and started pulling me away. I said, "Wait a minute. He didn't say or else yet." They started dragging me out of the courtroom, telling me that I was going to jail. I said, "Wait a minute man. I can't go to jail. I got to go to work."

When I was riding to the workhouse in the prison van I couldn't believe what was happening. Out of all of the criminal things that I had done since I had been to St. Louis, I couldn't believe that I was going to jail for some traffic tickets.

When they were processing me in, they assigned me to a counselor. I told him about my job situation and asked him what I should tell my boss. He came up with the dumbest answer I'd ever heard. He said, "Tell him the truth." I said, "ARE YOU CRAZY?" But I couldn't think of anything else, so I tried it. My boss told me that he would cover for me until I got out.

My two five day sentences ran concurrently, so with good time I only did three days. When I got out, J.R. picked me up.

I was still dating Johnnie Mae, but I started dating Jean, J.R.'s aunt at the same time. Nita's club, The Gaylarks, had another dance, and like I had done a few years earlier, I took two dates, Jean and Johnnie Mae. While we were there, Ralph introduced me to his girlfriend's sister. Her name was Sandi, and boy, was she fine. I spent most of the evening talking and dancing with her. She called me the next day and soon after that we started dating.

It was about that time that Ralph and I, along with our cousins Jug and Crow, started smoking Sherman Sticks. Sherman Sticks are Sherman cigarettes that had been dipped in PCP. Sometimes Ralph and I would sit on a bench at a bus stop on the corner of Jefferson and Cool Papa Bell, smoke a Sherman stick, and then try to find our way back to Wanda's house, which was two blocks away.

Shortly after that, my landlord said that we were going to have to move because she wanted to move back into that house. I knew she was lying. She had a big, beautiful house in Pagedale.

After we moved out, she rented the house to another family at twice the rent that we were paying. Mother moved into a senior citizens building, Ralph moved in with Wanda, and I moved in with Sandi.

Sandi was a very sweet and loving person, the kind of woman that any man would want. I really cared about her but she came into my life at the wrong time. After going through the pain of the break up with Gwen, I wasn't about to give my heart to anyone else anytime soon.

They decided to close the store where I worked. That meant I would soon be out of a job again. Dad called me and said that he had heard about what happened with the house and my job. God didn't tell him that time. Mother did. He asked me to move back to Chicago. He said that the flat upstairs, where I had grown up, was empty, and he really wanted me to come home.

I could hear something in dad's voice that told me that he needed me. I decided it was time to go. Sandi was hurt and disappointed when I told her that I was leaving. She tried to talk me out of it. She even cried and begged me not to go, but my mind was made up.

In the fall of 1983, six years after I had moved there, I said goodbye to everyone in St. Louis and headed back home to Chicago.

CHAPTER SIX

The Hoodlum Preacher

Christine decided to drive me to Chicago. She and Deborah had always been close, and they hadn't seen each other for a while. I tried to talk Ralph into going with me, but he didn't want to leave Wanda. No one in the family could stand the way she treated him, but he was too much in love to see how big of a fool he was. Chris decided to go with us to help with the driving. So, that Saturday morning, I packed up my few things and we headed down Highway 55 on our way to Chicago.

I admit I was a little nervous because I didn't know what to expect. When I had left six years earlier, I was wanted by the police for failure to appear in court for the bank case. And I didn't know what other lies Esther had accused me of after I stole all of her heroin. Although I had quit smoking about a year or so earlier, suddenly I felt like I really needed a cigarette.

When we got to Chicago, I did what I always did. I went to Dave's and got a polish sausage. Then we went to Deborah's and partied for a while. I went to Dad's, and he was glad to see me. He was living on the first floor where my grandparents had lived. I moved upstairs where I grew up.

Vernon still lived on Christiana, in the same building that he had grown up in. He worked at the Cook County Jail as a Deputy Sheriff, and was doing very well. I asked him to run my information to see if I had any warrants out for my arrest and he said that I was clean. No wants, no warrants. I was ready to make a brand new start in Chicago.

I was starting to think that I could be like everyone else. They had nice jobs, nice homes, nice cars, and they seemed to be so happy. That was the kind of life that I wanted. I was kind of like the fly that was trapped inside of a house. Everyday, he would look out of the window and see all of the other flies just flying around outside and enjoying themselves in the nice warm sun. He decided that he was going to get out of that house and enjoy the fresh air too. So he flew towards the daylight, only to bump his head on the windowpane. Again and again, he tried to break through, but again and again, he was blocked by the cold, hard glass. Eventually, he joined all the other flies that lay dead in the window seal. He did not have to die there because not far from the window was a door that was wide open and he could have flown safely through. But now he lay dead in the window seal because he was determined to do it his way.

We are often unsuccessful when we try to break free from situations in our lives because we are determined to do it our way. But what we don't realize is that there is a door nearby that is standing wide open. Jesus is that door. He is standing there with His arms open saying, "Come unto me, all ye that labor and are heavy laden, and I will give you rest." (Matt. 11:28)

Deborah was a big help to me. I wanted a telephone for my apartment, but didn't have a job. Deborah was manager of some doctor's office on 16th Street. I told the phone company that I worked there, and when they called, Deborah verified it. But we didn't stop with the phone company. I opened a credit account at Sears and got a 25-inch floor model television set.

I guess Ralph had finally had enough of Wanda's stuff, because about a month after I moved to Chicago, so did he. He moved into our old bedroom in the back, off the kitchen. I had our parent's old room, in the front next to the living room.

I got a job at J. C. Penney's at North Riverside Mall, working in home electronics during the Christmas season, and later moving over to the furniture department. Since I had worked for Penney's in St. Louis before the store closed, I counted that when it became time to apply for credit. Things were going great at work. I was one of the top salespeople, and with my commissions, I was making more money than I had ever made legally. I bought all new furniture for my apartment and a new TV set for Dad. I continued on my spending spree, buying several new suits, a gold chain, and even a diamond ring. Thanks to Deborah, I had the account at Sears, and had no problem getting whatever I wanted, including a fairly new 1981 Pontiac. I didn't have any problems getting ladies either.

Sheila was a cute, petite, dark-skinned, buxom, young lady with short hair. She, Ralph, and her sister Pat (who Ralph was crazy about) were drinking buddies. I met her when she came by the house to see Ralph one evening. We were drinking and smoking weed, and it was getting late. I was driving to St. Louis early the next morning, so I decided to go to bed. I asked Shelia if she wanted me to take her home, and she said no. When I asked her whether she was going to sleep on the couch or with Ralph, she said, "I want to sleep with you." That was the beginning of a three-year relationship. Although Shelia was generally sweet, she had a crazy side. Once, she was fired from her job as a bartender after threatening a female customer for talking to me.

Besides Shelia, I was also dating Fuzzy's cousin Beverly. I loved spending time with Beverly. If I had met her at a different period in my life, we probably could have had something special. But I was also dating a young lady from the neighborhood named Wanda, and another young lady who worked in the mall. I had a great job and was dating four beautiful, sexy women at the same time. I thought I was on top of the world.

Just when I thought it couldn't get any better, Nita and some of her club members came up from St. Louis for a weekend. My cousin Rose, ex-girlfriend Jean, and Royce, a woman I had been infatuated with for a long time, partied at my apartment for a while before heading out to Mom's on Roosevelt Road. The place was reminiscent of Mack's Lounge, their favorite tavern in St. Louis.

But the party soon took a sour turn. Jean became jealous of the way that I was slow dancing with Wanda and grabbed me by my tie. I didn't appreciate being fronted off, so I slapped her. Then Shelia said something to me and I slapped her too. Rose tried to calm me down. I left the tavern and headed for my car. Shelia knew that I was drunk, so she snatched my keys and refused to give them back. I kept hitting her, trying to make her give me the keys, but she wouldn't. I dragged Shelia down the street until Rose was finally able to pull me off of her, put me in her car, and drive off.

Rose tried to convince me that Shelia was right for taking my keys. I was too drunk to be driving. She talked me into going home with her, where I went to bed. She was right, but I was still mad.

The next day was Sunday. By the time I got to the west side, Nita and her club members were already heading back to St. Louis. Shelia came by and gave me my keys. And everyone on Christiana was talking about the wild night at Mom's.

141

I received a very pleasant surprise that summer. Jeri let the kids spend a few weeks with me in Chicago. I was glad to be able to spend some time with Andrea "Andi" and Everett, but I wasn't feeling as "fatherly" about Marcus. At first, I felt like he was being forced on me and I resented it. I think he sensed it and felt like he wasn't really wanted there. But the truth is, I was starting to like him. He was funny.

Andi celebrated her fifteenth birthday during their visit. I bought her a gold chain and French horn that matched mine. I think it was the first time that I had given her anything for her birthday. I had sent her a couple of Christmas gifts; but her mother refused to let her have one, and the other one was stolen.

I was proud of how well mannered Andi and Everett had turned out. But I couldn't take any of the credit for it. Jeri had done all that she could to raise those children, and I had done nothing. While she was busy trying her best to be a mother, I was busy trying my best to be a player. But I was glad that Jeri and I were able to be friends again.

I vowed that all of that was going to change. I was going to be a part of the children's lives and make up for the mistakes I had made in the past. I was going to be the best parent that I could be. It probably would have worked, had it not been for one very bad choice that I was about to make.

I took Andi and Everett to the bus station and saw them off. Marcus had gone on with Jeri about a week earlier. Later that evening I ran into Tadpole. He was on his way to Emma's house to shoot some boy (heroin). It had been a long time since I'd had any, so I decided to go with him. Emma lived with her mother and brother Joe. Her boyfriend, Q, was there too. I had not seen him since he had stolen my cocaine years earlier and gotten me busted. He denied tipping the police off about me, and since it had happened so long ago, we decided to let bygones be bygones. We all went into Emma's room and shot some heroin.

To this day, I don't know what possessed me to do such a thing. Why would I tempt the hands of fate in such a way? What was I trying to prove? I had shot dope off and on for over two years before I had gone into the Marines, and had seen first hand what it did to people. Everyone that I used to shoot up with back then was either strung out, dead, or in prison. But since I was able to quit, seemingly whenever I wanted to, I thought I could handle it.

But why would someone that had so much going for himself risk it all in such a way? What was wrong with me? Was I afraid of success? Was that why I chose the streets over my career, when I was moving up in politics? Was that why I chose to continue my criminal activities and risk my stripes, after I was promoted to sergeant in the Marines? And now, here I was at the top of my game as the number one salesman in the company, but the needle was calling my name again. And I chose to answer that call.

I stopped by Emma's the next morning and bought a dime bag. I shot it, and then went on to work. I started hanging with Tadpole more regularly, and we shot up almost every day.

One Saturday night, after I got off work, I wanted to get high. I couldn't find Tadpole, so I went to the spot to cop, myself. It was a dangerous place because it was in an alley, and they sold the drugs out of a rear window. No one with any sense went there alone at night. But I went anyway.

I tapped on the window, made my transaction, and headed back to my car. When I got close, I heard footsteps. I thought it was the slick boys, so I dropped the bag on the ground. When I looked up, I saw it wasn't the police. I spoke to the dude as he was coming towards me. Before I could do anything, I saw the gun in his hand. He put it to my head and said, "Give me the dope." I wasn't about to give him my drugs. That was my last ten dollars.

I stepped on the bag and told him that I had dropped it because I'd thought he was the police. He said, "Don't make me shoot you. Give me the dope." I said, "I told you, man. It's on the ground somewhere." He cocked the gun and said, "I ain't gonna tell you again. Give me the dope." I looked at him, wondering if I could take the gun from him without getting shot. But when I saw how badly his hand was shaking, I figured he was going to end up shooting me by accident. I took my foot off of the bag and said, "There it is, man. I told you I dropped it."

I was waiting for him to bend down to pick it up, so I could kick him in his head, but he told me to get in the car. I got in my car as fast as I could so I could run him over, but when I looked up he had disappeared. I drove around for about fifteen or twenty minutes looking for him. Finally I gave up and went home.

Tadpole came by about a half hour later. I told him what had happened. He said there was no way that I should have gone into that alley alone. All he had was $10.00, but he said he would split a bag with me. He said that it might be better if we got a bag of cocaine (Girl) instead of heroin (Boy). I had never shot cocaine before, so we decided to go ahead and get the Boy.

We went to a spot in K-Town, off of Roosevelt Road. I sat in the car while Tadpole went to the door. When he got back in the car and I pulled off, I saw a car pull out behind me. It was the Slick Boys. I sped up and turned the corner as fast as I could. Tadpole threw the bag out of the car before they could turn the corner. I drove about a half block before they pulled me over. They searched us, the car, and the surrounding area but weren't able to find anything. I dropped Tadpole off then went home mad as hell.

There was a big demand for hot (stolen) VCRs. Since I worked in the home electronics department at Penney's, I had access to lots of them. I solicited Emma and Q to help me get them out of the store. Since Emma knew the fence (buyer), it was a good partnership, for a while.

Two or three times a week I would give them three VCRs to take out. They sold for $600.00 each, retail. We got $200.00 for each one and split the take three ways. So with my paycheck ($500.00 to $800.00 per week in commissions during the peak season), and what I made from the VCRs ($400.00 to $600.00 per week), I was doing pretty well financially. But I was spending more money on heroin than I ever had before.

I was looking for some heroin one night, when I ran into Waynee, another dude from our block. He said that he was trying to cop too. But he also wanted some cocaine to mix with it and speedball. That was the second time I had heard of shooting cocaine, so my curiosity was peaked. I gave him $40.00 to go with what he had, and waited in the car for him to come back with the goods. He never did.

One thing that you learn early in the drug game is that you can't trust anyone. Even your "friends" will try to get over on you sometimes. They will do anything from watering down your part of the dope to disappearing with the money and telling you that they got ripped off or busted. Some of them will even go as far as keeping the drugs and giving you a counterfeit bag containing flour or something. Believe me, I know. I've done it all.

My heroin use had started getting out of hand. I was shooting $20.00 bags five or six times a day, everyday. I was afraid that the Jones (habit) had finally gotten me like it had gotten so many other people that I knew. But I had always been able to quit whenever I wanted, without going through the sickness or withdrawal pains that others went through. Even after shooting up for months at a time. But now, I wasn't just shooting up every day. I was shooting up several times a day, mainly because I could afford to. I had more money than I knew what to do with.

Some people, including Ralph and Shelia, started noticing a change in me. But more importantly, Dad noticed. His worst fear was that I would be a drug addict one day. When I was a child, he took me to see movies like "Monkey on My Back" and "The Man With the Golden Arm."

Dad may not have known that I was shooting dope, but he knew that something was wrong. Mainly, he knew that I was running from God. He would always tell me that I couldn't live or act just any kind of way that I wanted to. He said that I was a preacher and belonged to God.

Finally, I said, "Look Dad. I'm not a preacher anymore. I quit." He said, "Son, When God calls you to preach, you will always be a preacher. You're just a hoodlum preacher."

I decided, once again, that it was time to quit shooting heroin. But I was afraid to try. I was afraid that this time I would go through the withdrawals, and I didn't want to do that. When I was talking to another junkie about my dilemma, he said, "The best way to cleanse the heroin from your system is to shoot some cocaine." It made perfect sense to me, since heroin and cocaine were opposites.

When I got off of work the next evening, I went to Mom's and copped a quarter bag of cocaine from Saul Lee. I went home and dumped the whole bag into the cooker, put some water in it, and drew it up in the syringe. I went into the bathroom, found my favorite vein and shot it all at once.

It seems as though I heard a bell ring in my head. There was a feeling that came over me like I had never felt before. I got scared. My heart was rushing. My mind was rushing. My eyes were rushing. What had I found here? Dad hadn't told me about *this* before. This was even better than sex. While the needle was still hanging from my arm, I stuck my hand in my pocket to see how much money I had left. I had to get more. Now.

I thank God that Saul Lee's cocaine was not as potent as it should have been. Running a quarter bag like I did should have killed me. While I was walking back to Mom's to get another bag, I knew that I had finally met my match. Heroin couldn't do it. Marijuana couldn't do it. Not even alcohol could do it. But after shooting cocaine the very first time, I knew without a doubt that I was hooked, big time.

Shooting cocaine is nothing like shooting heroin. You might shoot heroin several times a day. If it is any good, you will never shoot it back to back. You will nod off for a while or get your sick off, and then get some more a few hours later. But as soon as you finish shooting cocaine, you want more. Sometimes people will shoot cocaine continuously for days at a time.

I made a lot of money at J. C. Penney's through commissions and my VCR sales. I always had several of my paychecks in my dresser drawer because I didn't need to cash them. When I started shooting cocaine, all of that changed.

My partner and I were selling more VCRs from my house than the salespeople at Penney's were selling in the store. I'd quit doing business with Emma and Q. Instead, I hooked up with Buck, Red's brother. He had recently gotten out of prison after doing a 10-year bit for murder. He was married and had a family, so he needed all the extra money he could get.

I added 5-inch, hand held television sets to my inventory. They were small enough for me to carry them out myself. I lined up several fences that I could take the "merch" (merchandise). Business was so good I couldn't keep up with the demand. My customers included policemen, business people, along with other crooks.

CHAPTER 6 - The Hoodlum Preacher

My biggest seller was the hand held TVs. I couldn't get enough of them. I always had a waiting list. My biggest fence, Maurice, who also supplied me with most of my cocaine, wanted all that I could get my hands on. But they were always out of stock. Management knew that things were coming up missing, but no one suspected me because I didn't work in home electronics anymore.

One day I decided to take the one out of the display case. I waited until the store was closing and the lights were out to make my move. I knew where they kept the key to the case, so I got it, opened the display case, took the TV out, and put the key back. I stuck the TV in my waistband and closed my jacket over it. I got on the elevator with the other employees and we headed upstairs to turn in our moneybags and clock out. The store's assistant manager was in the elevator too.

While we were in the elevator, I felt the TV starting to slide down my waist. I crossed my hands in front of me to keep it from sliding completely down my pants leg. It had slid too far down for me to walk, so when we got to the second floor as the elevator door was opening, I tugged up on the TV with my forearm trying to move it back into place. But when I tugged up on it, I accidentally hit the "on" switch, and the TV came on. Luckily, everyone was talking and walking out of the elevator, so no one heard the noise from the TV but me.

Instead of moving to the left with everyone else, I turned to the right and stepped into the men's room. I was lucky again. No one was in there. I reached down and turned the TV off. I stepped into one of the stalls and took the batteries out of it and put them in my pocket. Then I tucked the TV snugly into my waistband and left.

I was at my desk one day when a gentleman came over and introduced himself as the new head of security for the store. I got the feeling he was trying to tell me something. I should have listened. A few days later, Pat's boyfriend, Erwin, who was a regular Penney's shopper and a customer of mine told me that store security had called him asking questions about me. They told him that I was under investigation. He told me to be careful. I should have listened to him as well. By that time, I was too far-gone.

I was out of control. I was missing work for days at a time shooting cocaine all day and all night. When I did go to work, I would even shoot up in the men's room.

One evening, I decided to go to work and get more merch. I got to the store at about five o'clock that evening when I was supposed to have been there at noon. As soon as I got there, I went straight to the stock room to see if the shipment of VCRs had come in. It had. I called Buck, and immediately went to work.

I stashed five VCRs in different parts of the store. The crazy thing was that I saw some of the store's security officers peeking at me from around corners and behind counters, but I didn't care. I thought that I was slicker than them.

Buck got there shortly before the store closed. He had one of his sisters with him. I gave him two of the VCRs and told him that I would stop by his house later. They left.

At nine o'clock the lights started dimming, signaling that the store was closed. As usual, I started walking down the aisle toward the elevator. I saw the assistant store manager and one of the security officers walking towards me. I moved over to the next aisle and started walking down that one. They moved over to that one too. I knew it was over.

They asked me to go with them. When we neared the security offices, I saw that Buck and his sister had been apprehended. Sitting on the desk were two VCRs.

I later found out that they had gone through a lot of trouble to get me. They had been on to me for a while, but were unable to catch me. They had a security person whose assignment was to watch me. And the new head of security that had introduced himself to me a few weeks earlier had been brought in for one reason: to stop the one-man crime spree. Me.

Buck and I were arrested and charged with retail theft. They let his sister go. And since I wasn't at Penney's anymore, I had to come up with a new hustle. I started passing bad checks. I had heard during that time, that if you wrote a company in Illinois a bad check and they accepted a partial payment towards that check, they could not press charges against you. I didn't know how true it was, but I went with it.

CHAPTER 6 - The Hoodlum Preacher

My M.O. was to go into a store and purchase a TV, VCR, or other electronic item by writing a check. I only got top of the line merchandise, usually valued at $600.00 or more. I would sell it to one of my fences for one third of its worth. Then, a week or so later, I would call the store manager with a sob story, and make arrangements to pay off the check. Most of the time, I would give them $30.00 or $40.00 as a show of good faith, and tell them that I would pay the rest soon. But once they took the payment, I knew that they could no longer press charges against me. So they would never hear from me again. Hardly a day went by that I didn't write at least one check.

In spite of my drug addiction and criminal activities, I read the 121st Psalm every morning before I left home. Dad had asked me to start doing that a few months earlier, and it gave me a sense of comfort. Every morning I read the words, *I will lift up mine eyes unto the hills, from whence cometh my help. My help cometh from the Lord which made heaven and earth.* In retrospect, I think that was about the time that God started drawing me back to Him.

One night, Tadpole and I went back to the spot in K-Town to get some boy. He went to the door to cop, while I waited in the car. It is the person in the car's job to watch his partner's back while he is at the dope spot. He has to watch out for the Slick Boys and the stick-up man. Dope spots are the most dangerous places to be around at night because the stick-up man knows that you will be going in with money and the Slick Boys know that you will be coming out with drugs.

I was sitting there watching Tadpole on the porch. I was watching the surrounding area. At the same time, I was checking out all of the rear view mirrors making sure no one was sneaking up behind me. But when I looked in the driver's side mirror, I saw something that completely blew my mind. I saw the St. James Church of God in Christ, where I had been one of the associate ministers sixteen years earlier with my friends Campbell and Kennedy. My mind went back to those days when I was happy, praising God and being part of a church family.

I had almost forgotten that the radio was on, when I heard "I Want To Know What Love Is," a song that had been recorded by a group, Foreigner. They had a choir singing with them, so it sounded somewhat like a church song. As the song played, I cried.

Gotta take a little time
A little time to think it over
Better read between the lines
In case I need it when I'm older

This mountain I must climb
Is like a world upon my shoulders
Through the clouds I see love shine
It keeps me warm as I grow colder

In my life
There's been heartache and pain
I don't know
If I can face it again
Can't stop now
I've traveled so far
To change this lonely life

I wanna know what love is
I want you to show me
I wanna feel what love is
I know you can show me

Lord help me to be strong
On this road I travel on
When I'm lost and lonely
Find me
My journey's just begun
And I'm not the only one

I want to know what love is

    I sat there crying and wondering how I had messed up my life so badly. What had made me leave the church and people that I loved so much? What made me leave the people who loved me?

Why did I start traveling through this deep, dark dungeon of despair? I wanted out. Out of the lifestyle. Out of the drugs. Out of the streets. Out of the hustle. Out of the game. I wanted out now. I wanted to be back in church again.

I wanted to ask God to forgive me and give me another chance. But who was I fooling? I had messed up too badly. I had done too much wrong for God to ever forgive me. Not only was I strung out, but I had stuck needles in other people's arms, and had gotten them strung out too. There were women who had turned to prostitution so they could feed the habit that I had gotten them hooked on. It was too late for me. I had made my bed in hell, so I had to lie in it. Or should I say, die in it? That was what I thought.

I thought about a story that my father had once told me about a little boy who was trying to move a huge rock that was in his back yard. His father stood there watching his son struggle with the rock. Finally, the father asked, "Are you using all of your strength, son?" The little boy said that he was. The father watched his son a little while longer, before asking again, "Are you sure you are using all of your strength?" Once again the boy replied that he was. After watching his son struggle unsuccessfully for a few more minutes, the father said, "Son, I know that you are not using all of your strength, because you haven't asked me to help you." There are so many things that we struggle with in our lives, but we must realize that God is our strength and He is just waiting for us to ask Him for help.

I had been crying so hard, I hadn't seen Tadpole come back to the car. The stickup man could have dragged him off of the porch and into some alley, and I wouldn't have seen a thing except the St. James Church of God in Christ.

I thought it was too late to change, so I started running with another crew. One had just gotten out of prison. They called him Papa. He had a friend named Jerry living on Christiana who had done time too. We hooked up with Poopy who Tadpole and I used to buy heroin from years before and started getting high together.

Papa and I went to cop some boy and girl near 15th and Drake one night. Since he was on parole, I was the one who usually went inside. Had he been arrested, Papa couldn't have posted bond and gotten out of jail. He still would have had to stay in there until his court date. And even if found not guilty, still would have had to go back to prison to appear before the parole board and prove that there was no just cause for the arrest. If the board were to find that there was cause for the arrest, even though he had not committed a crime, his parole could be revoked.

We had already copped the boy from one spot and had gone to cop the girl. Papa waited in the car, holding the boy while I went in. I was walking through a gangway, heading to the car when I saw the slick boys pull up. When they got out of the car I put the cocaine in my mouth and started chewing it. They ran up to me and started choking me, trying to make me spit it out.

I kept trying to swallow it, and they kept trying to stop me. They flipped me onto my stomach and one of them jammed his knee against my back. Another one was choking me and saying, "Spit it out nigger. Spit it out." I finally got it down. I turned to them and said, "Too late." One of them said, "You think you did something slick don't you? I've got two bags in my car. And guess what? They're yours. They took me to jail and charged me with possession. Dad bonded me out the next day.

Another night, I parked my car in the alley behind my house. When I came out the next day, all four of my tires were flat. When I took one of the tires to the shop, the attendant told me that it was an ice pick hole. I knew that Poopy carried an ice pick all of the time, but didn't want to believe that he would do that to me. But I was told that earlier that morning he had been seen in the alley near my car. I took the tire iron from the trunk of my car and went looking for him.

I looked for Poopy for two days, with tire iron in hand, but I couldn't find him. Papa tried to talk me out of going to war with Poopy over something that was so silly. And truthfully, I really didn't want to fight Poopy. He was my friend. He had saved my life a few years earlier when I had shot an overdose of heroin. But I didn't know why he had stabbed my tires. And I wondered, if he had gotten the drop on me, would he have stabbed me too?

Finally, someone came to my house and told me that Poopy was outside, and wanted to see me. I grabbed my tire iron and went outside. We stood there staring at each other like two cowboys in a western movie. I had the tire iron in my hand and knew he had his ice pick in his. Oh, I forgot to mention something. Poopy was a big dude. I didn't want to fight him with just my fists, even if he didn't have an ice pick.

He said, "I heard you were looking for me." I said, "I heard that you flattened my tires." He said that he had gotten angry with me because I had gotten a large piece of cocaine but didn't give him any. He said that he had rung my bell, but I wouldn't answer the door. It had really hurt his feelings, so he stabbed my tires with his ice pick. The truth was, even though my car was there, I hadn't been home when he was looking for me. We apologized to each other and remained friends.

I had copped a one and one (one boy and one girl) one day and pulled up in front of my house when Don, Vernon's brother, came to the car and started talking to me. While we were talking, I glanced in the side view mirror and saw the slick boys cruising down the street. I held the drugs in my hand and watched them as they came closer.

When they got next to my car, I saw their doors opening. I threw the drugs in my mouth and started chewing and swallowing. They snatched me out of the car and started choking me. I thought to myself, "Here we go again." Just like before, I got it down. They handcuffed me and put me in their car, then searched mine. When they came back, one of them had a bag of weed in his hand and said that he'd found it under one of my seats. They arrested me for possession of marijuana.

While we were riding to the station, I remembered that I had my kit (needles, syringes, cookers, etc.) in my sock. I had just gotten them from my stash down the street, before I pulled up to my house. I kept trying to get it out of my sock without them seeing me, but I couldn't.

When we got to the station, they took me in and booked me. They were about to take me to the lock-up when one of them remembered that they hadn't searched me. He said, "If you have anything on you, tell us now. Because if you don't, and we find it, not only are we going to charge you with it, but we are going to bust you up."

153

THE HOODLUM PREACHER

Now, I had several syringes, two cookers (Richard's Wild Irish Rose tops), and some needles in a bulky paper bag stuffed down in my sock. Three big detectives surrounded me. They told me that they were going to hurt me real bad if they found anything on me. One of them said, "Last chance. Do you have anything on you?" I thought it over for a second or two, then said, "No."

Needless to say, they found my kit. You should have seen the looks that they gave me, and to each other. I was still handcuffed. My wrists secured behind my back, I fell back on the bench and started pleading. I said, "Hey man, I forgot I had that. I forgot I had that, man. I know y'all don't think I'm stupid enough to think y'all wouldn't find that stuff." Then I braced myself for the worst beating of my life. But they didn't beat me up. They just shook their heads and took me to the lock-up. Dad bonded me out the next day.

Another dude that I started running with was Big Red, another ex-con who was part of our "circle of friends." His hangout was a tavern named "The Bucket of Blood" on 16th and Kedzie.

One day, Ralph's girlfriend, Lavern, came to me with a proposition. Her sister and brother-in-law were selling cocaine out of their apartment. Lavern wanted to get some on credit, but they wouldn't give her any. So she wanted me to get some of my friends to stick them up. Now, that was not my M.O. I was a con man, not a stick-up man. Other than that night in San Diego when Williams and I went on our crime spree to recoup the money we had lost, I had never pulled a stick-up in my life. But I thought it would be a quick and easy way to get some dope and some money.

I told Big Red about it, and we decided to do the job ourselves. The plan was for Lavern to let me in the building to cop. I would trip the lock on the door when I went in, and Big Red would come in afterwards and rob everyone. But when we got to the door, he said that we were going to have to kill everybody in the house, including Lavern and any kids there.

I had never killed anyone in my life (that I know of) and couldn't go along with it. I told Big Red that the deal was off and walked away. I had done a lot of rotten things in my life, but thanks be to God, I couldn't do that.

154

I was arrested a couple more times and I was really getting tired of it. Besides, the charges from Penney's were still pending, and the likelihood of probation was fading fast.

One Sunday morning, I decided to go to my cousin, Rev. Ed Ivy's church. I had been ordained at Greater Mt. Calvary almost twenty years earlier, but by now they had moved to 16th and Cicero. Sheila and her daughter, Trina, went with me.

It felt kind of good to be in church. But when Rev. Ivy stood up to preach, he caught me off guard. He said, "We have a special guest here this morning." Then he said, "Rev. Barr, if you are Rev. Barr, please stand." I looked around, thinking that maybe Dad had come in. But he hadn't. He was talking to me. Nervously, I stood to my feet. Then he said, "Rev. Barr, if you are Rev. Barr, come to the pulpit." I went to the pulpit and took a seat.

It felt funny sitting in a pulpit again. I looked out at the congregation and recognized some people from my neighborhood, including Buck's mother and sister. What made it worse was they all recognized me too. After the sermon, I came forward and joined the church. What else could I do?

After service was over, Shelia started asking me all kinds of questions that I didn't have any answers to. Was I going to start preaching again? Did that mean we couldn't have sex anymore? What was going to become of us?

I started going to church pretty regularly. I was even helping out in the pulpit. I guess I thought that by joining church all of my problems would be over. My drug habit would just disappear. I would be Rev. Barr again, and things would magically return to the way they were in 1969.

It didn't happen. I continued with my same old routine, writing checks and taking the merchandise to Maurice or one of my other fences. Sometimes I would leave church and head to one of the malls or stores with my checkbook.

I came up with a plan. I called up one of the stores that I had ripped off and told the manager about my sales experience. I told him that if he hired me, he could keep half of my salary until my debt was paid. After that, if he liked the way I worked I would stay on. He said that he liked the idea and would contact me later that evening. I went home to wait for Shelia, smoked a joint, and started watching Smokey Robinson's show on TV with Ralph.

I was feeling pretty good. I had already passed a couple of checks that day, so I had a little money. Now it looked like I might be able to get a job and go legit. But I was fooling myself. There was no way that I could make enough money to support my habit by working a regular job, but I wanted to try. I never got the chance, though, because the doorbell rang, and when I went to answer it, it wasn't Sheila. It was the police.

Now you see what led up to my stay in the Cook County Jail, and how I became the Hoodlum Preacher. Sit back and relax while I tell you the rest of my story.

CHAPTER SEVEN

The Rescue

Division 4 was different from Division 2 in many ways. First, there were no dorms. Instead, there were two-man cells. There was no mess hall. All meals were brought to the wings on plastic trays. The gangs still ran the jail, but unlike Division 2, Peoples slightly outnumbered Folks.

There was a young brother named Will who called shots for Peoples in my wing. Folks was run by Gerard, an older brother around my age. I was put in a cell with another Neutron named Mitch, who was awaiting trial for possession of a stolen auto. Like all cellmates, we called each other "celly."

I got along well with everyone on my wing. Both gangs adopted me and treated me as one of their own. I didn't know it at the time, but God had His hand on me. It was because of His favor that I was treated as well as I was. Each gang had a "poor box" for their members who couldn't afford to buy cigarettes or snacks. I was welcome to get whatever I needed from either box. I didn't need much, though, because I made extra money by rolling cigarettes for both gangs.

There was a preacher named Rev. Hodges who came to the jail every Sunday night to conduct worship service. He would walk through the tiers and wings inviting the men to go to the service. I never went because I thought I had done too much wrong for God to forgive me. Every Sunday, when I saw him coming, I would go to the other end of the wing to escape him.

One Sunday, I was standing near the front of the wing talking to some of the brothers when I heard someone say, "Hey brother." When I turned around, Rev. Hodges was standing there. He said, "Why don't you come on down to the Bible study? God has got a word for you." I figured, What the heck? and told him that I would be there.

I went down to the room where the church service was going on and took a seat in the back. When Rev. Hodges started preaching, I noticed something almost immediately; he had that special something about him. I didn't know what it was, but I had seen it in Elder Campbell and Elder Kelly years earlier.

I sat up and started listening to what he was saying. He said, "I bet a lot of y'all are wondering why you are here in this jail. Some of y'all are here because, when you were on the street, doing your thing, God couldn't get your attention. He allowed you to be put some place to slow you down so that He can get your attention and you can hear Him. He does that because He loves you. Just remember, no matter what you have done or what you have become, God still loves you."

I left the service feeling better than I had in a long time. I realized that even with everything that I had done, God still loved me. I asked God to forgive me for all of my wrong doing. I asked Him to come into my heart and make me over in his image. After doing this, I felt a sense of peace come over me. Although I was still in jail, I felt as though I were free. Truly free. I had been rescued. Rescued from a life of misery and pain. Yes, I was free.

I started going to church every Sunday and taking other brothers with me. I also attended the services of a dear, sweet woman who came to the jail regularly, known as "Mother York." I read my Bible every chance I got. Before long, I was leading my celly and some of the other brothers in my wing in prayer and Bible study.

On Christmas morning, there was a special service in the gymnasium. Rev. Jesse Jackson and Mayor Harold Washington came with a delegation of dignitaries, including congressmen and local ministers. Rev. Jackson preached a good sermon, but I was most impressed that they had given up a portion of their holiday to encourage and inspire us.

I went to court for my fifth and final case in January of 1986. Auntee had gotten me a good lawyer. I was given probation on the previous four cases, but I was told that there was no way that I could win the fifth case. It carried a two to five year prison sentence. My attorney worked out a deal for me to plead guilty and get the lesser penalty of two years. If I went to trial and lost, I would get, at a minimum, four. With my record, maybe even five.

Besides, at that time, inmates in Illinois prisons were given "day for day". This meant, we would only serve half of our sentence. Therefore, if given a two-year sentence, I would only serve one. Since I had already been in the county jail for four months, I would only have to serve eight months in the penitentiary, minus any good time I received. I took it.

After sentencing, I was moved to maximum security. That was where Vernon worked. He came to see me sometimes and brought me cigarettes. I was only there for a week before it was time for me to be transferred down state. While we were passing through Division 5 to board the buses, I saw Maurice in one of the bullpens. For weeks I had been calling him, and leaving messages, asking him to bond me out of jail. I didn't know that he was in jail too - and in more trouble than I was. That just goes to show you how we sometimes place our hopes in the wrong people.

I spent about a month in Joliet, a diagnostic center where we were given all kinds of tests, before moving on to our respective institutions. I was given inmate number N60655 and sent to Centralia Correctional Center in Centralia, Illinois, which was about 70 miles north of St. Louis.

I continued going to church and studying my Bible, but I was disappointed that only a very few black churches visited with their ministry. Don't get me wrong, I know that God is not a God of color, and we were thankful for the white churches that came in, but there were times when we wanted to worship with people of our own race and culture. Sometimes, I longed to hear the soulful songs and the whooping sermons that I had grown up hearing. Most of all, I was starting to wonder if the black churches even cared about us. I thanked God that the white churches did.

I was walking around the yard praying one day when I heard God speak to me very plainly. He said, "Just as I sent Rev. Hodges into the jail to rescue you, I'm going to send you back into the jails and prisons to rescue others."

Since I was so close to St. Louis, mother and Sandi visited me regularly. My cousin, Crow, visited a few times as well. Before long, Buck was sent to Centralia, as were Cochise and my old celly, Mitch. Buck had beaten the J.C. Penney case because I had testified on his behalf and said that he didn't know what was going on. I claimed that I had tricked him when I'd called for him to pick up those VCRs. Like I said, Buck was a good friend with a wife and family to support. But he was at Centralia on a different case.

I decided that while I was there, I would go to school and continue my education. I enrolled in GED classes, studied hard, and applied myself. I ended up with the highest test scores in my graduating class. I still tell everyone that I was the class valedictorian of the state penitentiary. I immediately enrolled in the prison's college. Actually, all of the high school and college classes worked through the schools in the city of Centralia. Therefore, there is no indication on any of my transcripts that I was incarcerated during the time that I was a student. Although I learned a great deal by going to school, it was by listening to Oprah Winfrey and Bryant Gumbel of "The Today Show," that I learned proper grammar.

In July, I was released from prison and placed on parole. I was given $100.00 (minus my bus ticket), a shirt and pair of slacks, and was taken to the Greyhound bus depot. The officer waited until the bus departed. Finally, ten months after I was arrested, I was on my way home on a local. The bus stopped in every town between Centralia and Chicago. On one of the stops, I bought a 40-ounce bottle of beer and took my seat in the back. Since it was just beer, I didn't see anything wrong with it. I guess I had forgotten that drinking beer was how I began drinking and drugging in the first place.

Dad and Uncle Ray picked me up at the bus terminal when I arrived in Chicago. Boy, was I glad to be home! I hooked up with Ralph and some of my other friends on Christiana and drank more beer. I got together with Lavern's sister, Chocolate, to smoke weed and have sex. Later that evening, Sheila came by and we did the same thing. I was determined not to shoot boy or girl anymore.

I decided not to drink anymore and to get back involved in the church. Word spread around the church that I had just gotten out of prison and people started acting funny towards me, so I left. I wanted to find Rev. Hodges and join his church, but I didn't know how to locate him. I didn't know what church he was with or even his first name.

I started working with Ralph, renovating a building that Uncle Ray and Auntee had bought. It was near the one they lived in. They paid us each $30.00 a day. Ralph and I smoked weed and drank beer while we worked. I spent most of my money partying and buying clothes from Tadpole. Tadpole was working in the laundry at Cook County jail. He made extra money by cleaning, then selling the clothes prisoners had been wearing when they were arrested.

Eventually, I started hanging out with Papa, Poopy, and Jerry again. For some reason, I thought I could associate with them while they were shooting dope, and not shoot any myself. I was doing great, for a week or so. Before I knew it, I was hooked again.

It's kind of like a park that is located in St. Louis. Forest Park is very large and has many different roads, turns, and curves. One day, I decided to take a short-cut through Forest Park. When I got somewhere in the middle, I got lost. Every turn that I made was the wrong turn and every road that I took was the wrong road. Finally, I said, "Lord, if you will get me out of this park, I will never set foot in it again." A few weeks later, I was driving down a street that was close to Forest Park. I started thinking that I had gotten lost in the park the last time because I had gone too deep. I thought I could go back in as long as I was careful, watched where I was going and could see the main road, I would be OK. Besides, a lot of people drive through there without getting lost. So I ventured back into Forest Park. But the street that I was driving down turned into a one-way street, so I couldn't turn around. I found myself getting deeper and deeper into the park, and before I knew it I was lost again.

Satan tricks us that way sometimes. When God delivers us from things, instead of staying away from them, we think that we can flirt with them again. We fool ourselves into thinking that we can dibble and dabble as long as we don't go too far or get in too deep. We don't realize how quickly that road can turn into a one-way street. Before we know it, we are lost again.

One of the major problems with cocaine is it makes some people extremely paranoid; they begin seeing and hearing things that are not there. I had just finished shooting-up one night when I thought I heard something in Ralph's bedroom. He wasn't home, so I went in to take a look around. The power was off because we hadn't paid the electric bill, but we had a drop lamp in the kitchen that ran from the building next door. The cord wasn't long enough to reach all the way into Ralph's room, so I pulled out my Bic lighter.

After looking around the room and finding nothing, I decided to look under the bed. I got down on my knees and flicked my Bic. I couldn't see all of the way under the bed, so I put the lighter under the bed as far as I could reach. The box spring was old and ragged with loose strands hanging from the bottom. The flame brushed one of the strands, and the box spring caught on fire. I pulled the mattress aside and leaned it against the wall so that I could put the fire out. I didn't notice that the mattress was burning too. The flame quickly caught onto the curtains.

Eventually, I was able to put the fire out without any more damage. Dad came up and helped me carry the mattress and box spring to the alley. Ralph came home that night to see that he no longer had a bed anymore. Boy, I didn't think he could get that mad! I just thank God that I hadn't burned the whole house down.

Around this time, Fuzzy had moved into a small apartment on Pulaski near 15th Street. We started hanging out and getting high together. At first he was only drinking, smoking weed, and snorting cocaine, but before long, I had him shooting both cocaine and heroin. Interestingly enough, some of my old friends had not fallen to the needle or crack pipe. Vernon had bought a beautiful house on the south side, and Gip, although he had experimented briefly, was a supervisor for the phone company. We still saw each other from time to time.

One morning, Dad rang our bell and gave Ralph and me bad news; Uncle Ray had suddenly died from a massive heart attack. We all went over to console Auntee. It was that day that she made the biggest mistake of her life. She asked me to move in with her. I moved off of Christiana and into Auntee's apartment on Cermack, near Pulaski.

It was a large, three-story building with six apartments, three in the front and three in the rear. Auntee lived in front on the first floor, and her church was directly above her. She rented out the second and third floor rear apartments, and used the first floor rear and the third floor front apartments for storage.

She gave Uncle Ray's Eldorado to Ralph, while I drove their Lincoln Continental. The only problem was that Ralph didn't have a driver's license, and he never got one. The car just sat there on Christiana collecting parking tickets until the city eventually towed it away.

It didn't take me long to hook up with Linko, the neighborhood drug dealer, and the other neighborhood junkies. They said that I needed a nickname. My nickname was Bub, but they decided to call me "Preacher" because they said that I looked like a preacher. Although I didn't like it, I was stuck with the name Preacher, again. I guess Dad was right. I was a hoodlum preacher.

I still did a lot of business with Dennis, my regular dealer who lived on Douglas Boulevard, near Christiana. We had a code that we used when I was placing an order by phone. I would work a two-digit number into the conversation. The first digit let him know how many bags of boy I wanted, and the second digit was for girl. If I wanted two bags of boy and four bags of girl, I might say something like, "That shirt only cost 24 dollars," or "I think she's 24 years old."

I was getting ready to go cop one day when Auntee asked me to go to the grocery store for her. I decided to go to the store first so I could take my time doing my thing. When I got there, I saw a young man standing outside hustling money to bury his young daughter who had recently died. He even had a picture of her. I was touched so deeply that I gave him my cop money. I figured I could always get more money. A few months later, I saw him standing in front of the same store with that same picture and that same sob story. I was so angry that I grabbed him by his collar and took back the $20.00 that I had given him.

My drug habit started to increase like it had before. Rose had been strung out on cocaine before, so she knew what I was capable of. To support my growing habit, I started running con games on Auntee and stealing things out of her house. Rose tried to tell her that I needed to go into a drug program, but she wouldn't listen. Auntee had two full-length mink coats; I stole both of them.

One Saturday, night I was rummaging through some drawers when I ran across Dad's tithes envelope that he had brought over for church the next day. I opened it and found $40.00. I took the money and resealed the envelope, knowing I couldn't get away with it, but at the time, not caring. I had to have it.

When Dad and Auntee confronted me the next day, I told them about my habit and that I needed help. I enrolled in a treatment program at a rehab center near Chinatown. It was a seven-day program, but I left after only three. The reason I went in the first place was to get them off of my case. Unfortunately, this is the reason a lot of people go into rehab or treatment programs; either to keep from going to jail or to appease their family members.

When I left rehab, I went back to my same old routine. Mom's was always packed on Wednesday nights because drinks were two for one. I was standing at the bar one evening, when I heard a familiar voice. I turned around and saw Waynee standing and talking to someone. I grabbed him by his throat and started choking him. The bartender saw this and warned us to, "Take it outside."

I pulled Waynee out of the tavern and said, "Give me my money." His friend tried to step in, but I pointed to him and said, "You ain't got nothing to do with this." Waynee started telling me some story about how he got busted. He promised to pay me as soon as he got it, but I knew he was lying. I took the few dollars that he had and told him to get out of my face.

One Sunday night, I really needed some money. I decided to go to St. James Church of God in Christ and try to run a con on Elder Campbell. When I went in, he was preaching. I sat at the back of the church and waited until he finished. Afterwards, I went up to him and gave him a sob story. He told me that he was glad to see me, but that he didn't believe a word that I had said. I don't know whether God told him that I was lying or if I just looked like I was. He took me by the hand and said, "I'm praying for you." I went home angry. I didn't want any prayer. I wanted some dope.

In January of 1987, I went and got a one and one. On the way home, I decided to buy a new outfit (syringe and needle) to shoot it with, so I went to Big John's. We'd had a snowstorm a few days earlier, so parking spaces were limited. While I was squeezing into a parking spot, I noticed the Slick Boys sitting in their car waiting for me to finish parking. I decided to wait them out.

I maneuvered my car back and forth, acting like I was trying to get closer to the curb. All of a sudden, I heard someone tapping on the window. I turned around and saw one of them standing there with his badge out. I had stashed the boy before reaching Big John's, but I still had the girl in my hand.

I sat there trying to decide what to do with the dope. The package was too big and had too many staples in it for me to try to swallow it. I thought about opening it and smashing the contents into the carpet. I didn't know what I would do, but I knew what I wasn't going to do. I wasn't going to open the door, and they couldn't make me. While I was deciding what to do, the door opened-I had forgotten to lock it.

They took me to jail and charged me with possession of a controlled substance. I stayed in the Cook County jail until I went to court. The arresting officers didn't show up in court so the charges were dismissed, but I still had to go back to Joliet because I was on parole. I was back to being inmate number N60655.

After a week of processing, I was taken downstairs to await transportation so that I could be taken across the street to general population. I was sitting on the floor, chained and shackled to some other prisoners, when I heard a familiar voice. I couldn't see who it was, but what he said sounded very familiar.

"You know, there are two kinds of people in this world, the players and the squares. The squares are at home with their families right now. They're eating what they want to eat, going where they want to go, and doing what they want to do, whenever they want to do it. But us players, we're sitting here on this cold, hard floor, chained up like a bunch of animals. We got somebody telling us where to go, what to eat, when to eat, and when to sleep." Then he said, "I don't know about y'all, but whenever I get out of here, I'm gonna be a square. Cause I ain't gotta live like this."

I was tired of living like that too. I was hurting myself. I was hurting my family. But for some reason, I couldn't stop. I felt helpless and hopeless, and I blamed everybody. I blamed Dave for accusing me of stealing from Woolworth's when I hadn't taken a dime. I blamed Claude for getting me to start smoking weed. I blamed Tadpole for getting me to start shooting heroin. I blamed

165

those church folks for the way they treated me when I'd gotten out of prison. I blamed Nelson, Jeri, Thad, Papa, Poopy, the Marines, the police, the school system, and everybody else. My life was miserable. I was completely out of control, and I blamed everybody but myself for making me that way. Yeah, it was everybody's fault but my own.

I wrote Andi a letter while I was locked down. She wrote back and I was happy and surprised to hear from her so quickly. What she wrote really forced me to think. She asked, "Dad, why is it that the only time you write me is when you are in jail?"

She was right. That was the only time I wrote anyone. It's what happens when someone gets locked up. They start writing to everyone and get angry when people don't respond. They forget that it is their lives that are on hold and not everyone else's.

I went before the parole board, they ruled in my favor. I was released from prison, but when I got home, I learned that Auntee had knew that I had stolen Uncle Ray's last social security check and forged his signature. She also knew that I had stolen his credit cards and used them, then sold then to Big John. I convinced her that I had changed since going back to prison.

But that was short lived. I found her church's old checkbooks from a closed account, forged some checks in my name and cashed them. I conned some of her church members out of money too. To make matters worse, Linko and some other dealers had started coming around looking for me because I owed them money.

Auntee and I were sitting in the living room arguing one day when I noticed a blank stare on her face. She stood up, walked over to the hall closet, reached up to the top shelf, and brought down a gun. She walked towards me, almost in slow motion. She pointed the gun at me and said, "You no good bastard. There's just no good in you."

I jumped up, started backing out of the room and begging her not to shoot me. When I got out of the living room, I ran out the back door. I kept going until I was on Christiana. I had never seen Auntee look like that before. I had never seen anyone look like that. I'd never even heard her curse.

166

I stayed gone until the next day. When I went back, I apologized to her for stealing all of her stuff and selling it. Unfortunately, she had made a mistake by not shooting me when she had the chance. As soon as I could, I stole her gun and sold it.

The words of The Stylistics' 1972 record, "Children Of The Night" often played through my mind. Although The Stylistics weren't talking about drugs in the song, that was how I felt. I had become one of the children of the night who was constantly in search of the company that I craved so badly. Cocaine. In a sense, all street hustlers fit into that category. It doesn't matter whether they are pimps, prostitutes, drug dealers, drug users, players, or player haters. They roam the streets at night, in search of whatever they need to get by.

One night, I went down near Homan to cop at a drug house on Polk. The drugs were sold from the third floor apartment, but the dealers controlled the entire building. As I walked up to the building, I saw a tall, light skinned dude get out of a car across the street and start walking toward the building too. While I was walking up the stairs, I heard someone come in behind me. I figured the man was there to cop too.

I finished taking care of my business and headed down the stairs. It dawned on me that the dude had never come upstairs. I hadn't heard him leave or enter any other apartment. Something was wrong.

I stuck the drugs and my money into my jock shorts. I continued walking down the stairs and saw him standing between the first and second floors with a shotgun. He jammed the gun into my stomach and told me to give him my money and drugs. I told him that I didn't have anything. He said he knew that I either had some money or some dope, and that I had to give it up. I told him that I didn't have any money, that I had gone up there trying to get a bag on credit but had been turned down.

He told me to follow him outside to his car so that he could search me. He had to be crazy. As soon as the man turned his head and started down the stairs, I took off up the stairs, yelling and banging on doors. He ran down the stairs and out of the building. Some of the guys came into the hall, and I told them what had happened. Since I was one of their regular customers, they made sure that I got out of the area safely.

A few days later, Mother called asking what was going on. She said that Dad had called her and told her that I was doing wrong. He'd said there was no good in me at all. It had become apparent that I had really hurt two of the people who loved me the most, and had always been in my corner.

But Dad couldn't stay angry with me. He prayed for me continually and never gave up. He called me early one Saturday morning to see how I was doing. After we talked for a while, he said that he was going to pick up some groceries. I knew that the closest grocery store was about six or seven blocks from his house. I asked him if he wanted me to take him to the store but he said, "Naw Son. You know that's how I get my exercise." We talked a while longer, and then said our good-byes.

A few hours later, Ralph and I were doing some work on the building next door. I decided to go to the dope spot on Polk and Homan to get a one and one. Instead of driving, I caught the bus, so Auntee wouldn't know that I was gone.

Riding back, I noticed an ambulance and a crowd of people on the corner of Roosevelt and Christiana, but I couldn't see what had happened. When I returned to the house, I told Ralph that something bad had happened near the crib. While we were talking, Auntee dropped in to say that someone was at her house and wanted to talk to us. We were told that Dad had been run down by a hit and run driver on his way home from the store.

I was given the cross that he had been wearing. He had been hit so hard that the chain had been knocked across the street. They took dad to Mt. Sinai, the same hospital where Andi had been born. He lay there in a coma. I went to see him everyday, but Auntee stayed beside her little brother around the clock.

One day, I needed some money for dope. I called Miss Frankie, one of Auntee's church members, and told her that Auntee had just called to tell me that Dad was doing better, but she needed some money for something. But she said, "Rev. Rayford just called me and said that Rev. Barr has died."

Dad was dead. I walked the streets crying and thinking about my best friend. I was almost in shock; I couldn't believe it. I knew that he had been in a coma, but I thought he would come out of it and be all right. I had planned to take him home and care for him. Now, he was gone. My dad was gone.

Dad had died shortly after Mother's Day in 1988. His funeral was held at my cousin Lee Howard's church on Roosevelt, near California. Mother, Nita, Christine, and Christaball drove in from St. Louis, and Andi and her cousin Kelli drove in from Detroit.

A few weeks after Dad died, I rented his apartment to Dennis to sell drugs out of. God must not have been pleased with that because it got robbed the very first night that it opened. A few days later, Vernon told me that he knew what was going on and that he and the people on Christiana weren't going for that, especially in Rev. Barr's house. We closed shop.

Mother thought it would be good for me if I got out of Chicago and went to St. Louis for a while. With me owing Linko and a few other dealers money, I thought it might not be a bad idea. Besides, I was ready to leave the heroin and cocaine alone. Standing at his gravesite, I had promised Dad that I would.

I was in St. Louis for about a week when I decided to stay there. I hadn't shot any drugs since leaving Chicago and I was starting to feel good. I called Auntee, apologized for all of the things I had put her through, and asked her to send my clothes. This time it wasn't a con. I was truly sorry and meant every word.

I stayed with Mother for a while, sleeping on her couch. She lived in a senior citizens building near Jefferson and Cass, and according to the rules, the residents' guests were only allowed to stay for two weeks. I stayed an extra week, with permission from the building manager. It had been almost three weeks since I had done any drugs and I was feeling good.

One Wednesday night during those first three weeks, I decided to go for a walk. I bought a 7-Up from a corner store, walked to the bus stop on Jefferson and Cool Papa Bell and sat on the bench where Ralph and I used to sit and smoke PCP. After sitting there for a while, I began noticing cars pulling up, parking, and people getting out and walking down the street. I sat there praying and thinking. More and more cars pulled up, until pretty soon the lot was full and people had to park on the streets. I started wondering, "What's going on and where are all of these people going?" When I looked around, I saw them going into a church, the Morning Star Missionary Baptist Church.

I wondered what could be going on in that church on a Wednesday night that attracted that many people. It couldn't be a worship service, because no one was dressed up. Finally, my curiosity got the best of me and I went in. I don't know what I was expecting to see, but what I saw completely blew my mind. The church was jam-packed, on a Wednesday night, for a Bible study class. I found a seat in the back and sat listening.

The pastor was a very good teacher, but there was something more to him. He had that same thing that I had seen in Elder Campbell, Elder Kelly, and Rev. Hodges. What was it? And why did some preachers have it while others didn't? Maybe other preachers did have it, but whatever "it" was, just wasn't as powerful in some as it was in others.

I went up to the pastor after the class was over and introduced myself. I told him how I had enjoyed his teaching. He introduced himself as Freddy Clark, and invited me to worship with them again. I went back on Sunday morning and had a great time. He was a very powerful preacher.

My three weeks at Mother's apartment ended and I eventually had to leave. Uncle Johnny had died from a stroke a while back and Christine and her children were living in Aunt Nini's basement. Christaball, a master carpenter, had converted the basement into a two-bedroom apartment. I slept on the couch in their living room for a couple of nights, until Aunt Nini found out and told me I had to leave. She didn't want me staying there. I moved into Bobby and Irene's basement. Bobby worked the night shift at the railroad, and Irene drove a bus for Bi-State, the St. Louis area's bus company.

I started going to Morning Star Missionary Baptist Church because I really enjoyed Pastor Clark's preaching and teaching. But Bobby and Irene were members of Solomon's Temple on Page Boulevard. I went to church with them sometimes, and they eventually convinced me to join, but I felt a connection with Pastor Clark. After several weeks of attending both services, I joined Morning Star as well. I was a member of two churches.

170

I thought that since I was licensed and ordained as a minister, and wasn't drinking or drugging anymore (I had been clean for five weeks), I was supposed to be a preacher. I told Pastor Clark that I was a preacher and showed him my credentials. He welcomed me with open arms. But truthfully, I didn't really want to preach anytime soon. I just wanted to sit under him and learn as much as I could. Then, maybe one day, I would possess whatever it was that he had.

Unfortunately, Bobby and Irene wanted me to go to church with them too. Although Bobby and Irene were serious about church, they were still drinking and smoking weed. So, I compromised. Sometimes I went to Morning Star, while on other days I attended Solomon's Temple with them.

I'm not taking anything away from Solomon's Temple or the pastor, Bishop Holloway. He was a powerful preacher too. But I believe that God sent me to Morning Star because He had given Pastor Clark the message that I needed to hear at that time, and He knew that I would identify with him more.

I got a job at Sears, selling home electronics part time at the Jamestown Mall. I didn't have a car, so I couldn't make it to Bible study anymore, however, I was at Morning Star every chance I got. Christine's daughters, Tenesha and Tawana, started attending with me.

One day, Pastor Clark told me that he wanted me to preach at the early morning service. I was scared to death. Sitting in the pulpit was one thing, but actually preaching a sermon was something completely different. It had been nineteen years since I had preached.

Luckily for me, the early morning service began at 7:00 a.m. and only a handful of people were there. I made one or two theological errors, and Pastor Clark corrected me on them. Other than that, I think I did all right, but I knew I had a lot to learn. And I figured that I could learn best from Pastor Clark.

To be honest, I was no more ready to be in that pulpit than I had been to preach again. I wish now that I had told Pastor Clark about my not-too-distant past, and the challenges that I was going through living with my cousins. Maybe he could have helped me avoid some of the pitfalls that were ahead of me. Maybe he could have kept me from returning to the lifestyle that I had already been rescued from on two occasions. Maybe things would have been different had I just talked to him. Maybe. Just Maybe.

I was like a lot of other church folks. I was using the closet for the wrong reasons. When I was a child, I hid the things that I didn't want my parents to see, in the closet. Anything that I was not supposed to have, such as cigarettes, dirty magazines, or things that I had stolen, were all hidden in the closet. Jesus said that we should use closets to pray, meaning we should pray in private. I, however, was hiding my sins in the closet. There are a lot of "closet-sinning Christians" in our churches. There are closet alcoholics, closet drug addicts, closet adulterers, and closet gamblers. We hide our sins and weaknesses in the closet because we don't want other church folks to know we are not as holy as they might think. Jesus knows and loves us anyway.

CHAPTER EIGHT

<u>The Renegade</u>

Irene started taking me to Danny's with her after church and buying Sherman Sticks. I don't know where she knew Danny from, but he had a drug house on Taylor, near Page. Although Danny sold Sherman Sticks, the majority of his business was crack. It wasn't long before Irene and I made the transition from smoking sticks to smoking crack. Bobby, though, was trying to get closer to God. Having never really been into drugs, he smoked a little weed every once in a while, but stuck mainly to beer.

Pretty soon, I started missing work again. This time to get high with Irene and her friends. Sometimes we would go to one of their houses, but mainly we got high in Irene's basement where I lived. Ironically, I had left Chicago to get away from the heroin and cocaine, moved to St. Louis, and now I was smoking crack. It seemed to be a more sociable way of getting high than sticking a needle in an arm and bleeding all over the place. Plus, there were always plenty of women around, who were sometimes quite "freaky."

Thinking back on it, it was about that time that Andi was in that automobile accident back in Detroit. I had talked to her on the phone a couple of times, but my part time job didn't allow enough money to go there. I honestly didn't know how badly she was hurt. Had I known, I would have found a way to get the money.

Before long, I was hooked on crack. I started stealing items from Sears and selling them to Danny for drugs. Sometimes I used Chris to help me get some of the merchandise out of the store. Eventually, I was caught, arrested, and then fired. To get the amount of money that I needed, I went back to doing what I did best: passing bad checks.

I hit stores all over St. Louis, knowing that there was no way I would be able to fix the mess that I had gotten myself into. I was in a lot of trouble, and there was no way out. I called Sandi to tell her that I had gotten myself into some trouble that I couldn't get out of. I told her that I was scared, really scared. I was almost in tears. She talked and tried to comfort me the best that she could, but we both knew that I was out of control.

THE HOODLUM PREACHER

I found a job at Famous Barr department store in downtown St. Louis. Every day took hundreds of dollars from the cash registers to spend on crack. When I arrived at the store one Saturday, the security officers were waiting for me. They walked me into the office and informed me that they knew what I had been doing. I was asked to sign a confession, but I refused.

I wasn't arrested because I had been careful to leave no proof of my thefts. I knew where the security cameras were and had always positioned myself where I couldn't be seen or taped. Still, after working there not even an entire week, I was fired.

To add to the problem, the license plates on Irene's pick-up truck had expired. She had a warrant out for her arrest, so I was doing all of the driving. It was the least that I could do, since I couldn't pay any rent. One day, I was supposed to take Irene someplace. As soon as I pulled onto the street, an officer pulled me over. He ran a check on me and found that there was a warrant out for my arrest. I was on my way back to jail. By that time, I saw going to jail as an occupational hazard.

On Super Bowl Sunday 1989, I wanted to make some money so that we could get high. I decided to take a 25-inch TV to my fence before the game started. Because Irene was cooking, she couldn't go with me; but she let me use her truck. I didn't know how to get to the Galleria Mall, but Chris did, so I picked him up.

We reached the mall shortly after noon, and I knew that it would only take a few minutes to get the TV. I left the keys with Chris and asked him to pull the truck up to the curb when I came out. I brought out the TV, but Chris was nowhere in sight. I carried the TV to the truck and found the door unlocked. The TV wouldn't fit in the truck's cab, so I put it on the back and waited for Chris to return.

I figured that Chris was in the mall somewhere, but I couldn't just leave the TV on the back of the truck and go looking for him. I waited, and waited, and waited. When the mall closed, Chris still hadn't come back. The parking lot began to empty, and before long I was alone.

I walked to a nearby pay phone and started calling people, hoping that someone could pick me up. Irene couldn't leave yet, and everyone else was watching the Super Bowl game. So I went back to the truck to wait for Chris to return with the keys. It had begun to get very cold inside the truck. I sat shivering from the cold and steaming with anger.

I returned to the pay phone, but I still couldn't get anyone to come for me. I considered leaving the truck and TV there and catching a bus home, but I didn't have any money and had no idea which bus to catch. So I waited. After a while, I saw a pick-up truck coming towards me. The closer it got, the better I could see the two white guys inside. They looked at me then circled my truck and drove off. I had a feeling that I hadn't seen the last of them, so I searched the truck for anything that could be used as a weapon. I found a tire iron and rested it across my lap.

I was right. Half an hour later, the men were back. They circled my truck again, then stopped and sat looking at me for a few minutes. They got out and came towards me carrying two by fours. I picked up the tire iron and waited. I knew that I was in trouble, but no way was I going out without a fight.

Just as they reached my door, I saw a car speeding across the parking lot towards us. I thought some of their friends had come to join the party, but I was wrong. Irene and Janet, a bus driver friend of hers, jumped out of the car carrying baseball bats. I got out of the truck with the tire iron and Irene hollered out, "What do y'all want to do?" The men jumped back in their truck and sped off. I had never been happier to see anyone in my life.

Irene, Janet, and I took the TV to one of my fences and sold it for $200.00. We used part of the money to buy crack from a dude on the street, but it turned out to be a piece of soap. That's the way the game goes. I have sold lawn grass to people who were looking for marijuana, and baking soda to people looking for heroin or cocaine. We gave the rest of the money to one of our regular dealers, then went to Janet's house and got high. Sometimes when you are trying to get some fire drugs, you end up getting burned instead. Later, Chris came up with some jive story about what had happened to him, but everybody knew that he was lying.

Weeks later, Irene and I went to Sears on South Grand. I had already hit the store once, but sometimes I would hit the same store two or three times in a week. While I was waiting for approval on the check that I had written, I saw one of the security officers enter the manager's office. I knew then that they were on to me. I started looking for a way out. There was none.

I was arrested, handcuffed, and taken away. They didn't know that Irene was with me, so she was allowed to leave. After they put me in the squad car, one of the officers turned to me and said, "Stay off of the South Side." Then he said, "Naw. You get out of St. Louis and don't come back." He looked at me really hard and asked, "Did you hear me? Get out of St. Louis, and don't come back. You better not even show up in court." Then they took me to jail.

While I was being processed, one of the detectives asked if I had ever been arrested. I knew that he was going to check my rap sheet, but said, "No." I learned long ago, never tell on myself. He put my information into the computer, and I thought that thing was never going to stop printing. He turned around, and his look said it all. "I thought you said that you had never been arrested." What could I say? "Oh. You said 'arrested'?"

I got out of jail the next day, and knew that I had to get out of town. The police had made that very clear. But I didn't have anywhere to go. I couldn't go back to Chicago or California. I called Jeri, talked to her about possibly moving to Detroit, and she said that she would help me get situated. Every time I got the money together, I messed it up right before I was supposed to leave.

One night when I was on my way to pick up a large quantity of cocaine, I tried to make a left turn before the light turned red. I didn't make it. As I was turning the corner, I saw a police car sitting there. The emergency lights began flashing, and my heart sank into my stomach. I had missed all of my court dates, and truly believed that I would be on my way back to jail, but the car turned and sped off in the other direction. I decided at that moment that I wouldn't take any more chances. So that February, I left St. Louis for Detroit.

Once in Detroit, I moved into Jeri's sister Lois' spare bedroom. I had always gotten along well with her and her son Darnell. I took a job at Robinson's Furniture, and to be near Andi,

I started attending the Indiana Avenue Church of God in Christ on Indiana Avenue and 8 Mile Road. I eventually joined.

I still thought that since I was licensed and ordained in the ministry, I was supposed to go in as a preacher when I joined a church. I also thought that by joining a church I would automatically be transformed into a "Super Christian." I went to Indiana Avenue as Elder Barr, since I had been ordained an elder in the COGIC. But I no longer had my credentials from the COGIC, and the pastor, Elder Evans, wanted me to get a letter verifying my ordination. I knew that getting a letter would be next to impossible because Bishop Campbell had died, and the last time I had seen Elder Campbell had been when I was high and trying to con him out of enough money to buy more drugs.

Neither Jeri nor Andi was happy about my decision to join the church. Jeri was unhappy about the church being COGIC. She still didn't care much for them, and at the time Andi didn't have care much for me. I couldn't blame her.

Before long, I moved in with another of Jeri's sisters. Myra and her husband Reggie had a big, beautiful home. They accepted me as part of the family. At the time, Jeri was still living with her significant other, but was supposedly working her way out of the relationship with him so that we could try to be a family again. To tell the truth, I didn't go to Detroit to reconcile with Jeri. I went there because I didn't have anywhere else to go.

Reggie helped me get a job at Capitol Building Supply Company as a forklift driver and yard worker. I was happy to have the new job, since the manager at Robinson's Furniture and I argued constantly. I had never in my life been on a forklift, but I practiced during my lunch hour when no one was around. After a while, I got to be pretty good.

A few weeks after I started working at Capitol, the yard foreman quit, and I was promoted to his job. On a day when we were short on delivery drivers, I loaded up one of the flatbed trucks and took it out myself. No, I had never driven a big truck before. I didn't have a driver's license, and didn't know my way around Detroit; but I wanted to get out of the yard for a while, so I didn't tell anyone. Most of the time I drove around lost.

THE HOODLUM PREACHER

Jeri, Marcus, and I moved into an apartment on Cortland Avenue. Marcus and I started bonding, and I really took a liking to him. It no longer mattered whether or not he was my biological son. It no longer mattered whether or not Jeri had had an unusual pregnancy. Maybe she really had been pregnant for more than nine months. Marcus had nothing to do with that, and he had nothing to do with whatever problems Jeri and I had. He was a good kid and as far as I was concerned, Marcus was my son.

I bought a car so that we could have transportation, and things began to look up for us. The good times didn't last long. Our gas was turned off because of an unpaid bill. Since it was still summer, we weren't bothered much. After a while, I started hanging out with Greta, one of Jeri's friends. It was worse than a romantic or sexual relationship. We got high together. At first, we were just drinking and smoking weed together, but it wasn't long before I was smoking crack with Greta and her friends.

News soon came from St. Louis. Bobby had died suddenly, and unexpectedly. I didn't go back for his funeral, but had no doubt that he was with the Lord because he had always prayed for Irene and me. Despite Bobby's struggle with alcohol, and his inability to attend church as much as he liked, his faith in Jesus Christ had never wavered. I soon left the church again.

Unlike before when God had placed people like Rev. Hodges, Rev. Clark, and my father into my life to lead me back to Him, this time I was alone. Before, they had worked to let me know that my life was not my own. I belonged to God. I was His property. Yet, I was a renegade. A defector. A deserter from the army of the Lord.

I started doing more drugs, even getting high while at work. One day, I borrowed a co-worker's car during my lunch hour so that I could go and cop. It was a new car, and I wasn't familiar with the alarm system. I left the dope house with three bags of heroin and five rocks of crack in my hand, opened the car door, and the alarm went off. I couldn't stop it. A police car made it's way down the street towards me. I was relieved to see it keep moving. I lifted the hood and disconnected the alarm.

I had forgotten how cold Detroit winters could be. The gas was off again, so the house was freezing. A couple of space

178

heaters helped some, but the heat wasn't working in the car either, and I worked outside. I was cold.

I was, again, fired from my job because of my drug habit. I had started stealing from the yard and selling merchandise on the side. But that wasn't what led to my unemployment. I was fired for stealing the company's pick-up truck one night and keeping it all weekend to deliver stolen goods.

To make money, I again went back to passing bad checks. I told Jeri and Marcus that I was working at night, but I was really hustling and drugging. One Friday, I stayed out all night getting high with Greta and some of her friends. The next day, as I was getting ready to go home, Greta asked me to take her to get some more drugs. I didn't want to. I was tired, sleepy, and ready to go home, so I pulled off of the road and told her that I was going home. She kept trying to talk me into taking her to cop again.

All of a sudden, two cars boxed me in. At first I thought it was the police. But it was worse. Jeri, Andi, Marcus, Myra, and a few other people got out with bats, sticks, and two by fours and began pounding on the car windows. I was so high, I couldn't tell who was there or what was going on.

Greta was freaking out, screaming and hollering, and telling me to drive off, but I just sat there looking at them. Not that I was too cool to be afraid, I was just so high that I didn't care. I couldn't care. I think Andi was the only person not swinging anything. I think, but to be completely honest, the only thing I remember about the incident was looking at Andi and saying, "You never gave me a chance to explain."

After everything was over, I drove back to Greta's house. Maybe an hour later, Andi called asking me to come home so that we could talk. She was concerned about the shattered windows and asked me not to drive my car, but I was hard headed. When I got home, Jeri, Andi, and I talked for a long time. They actually thought that Greta and I were having an affair. I told them that we weren't, but I also told them that we weren't doing drugs. I denied anything involving drugs. I just wanted it to be over.

My crack habit was worse than ever. I was smoking everywhere and all of the time: In the basement, in the car, in the park, walking down the street. I was even smoking in the bathroom while Jeri and Marcus were home. I passed checks for computers, microwaves, and anything else that my clientele wanted. Word that I could get anything soon spread, but no one knew how I was doing it.

Even though business was good, I knew it couldn't last forever. I had passed too many checks around Detroit. I knew that the law would catch up with me sooner or later. So I decided to make my biggest sting of all, then get out of town.

Since people believed that I could get anything, I decided to use the lie to my advantage. I told everyone that I would be picking up a load of merchandise on Saturday night. I said that I would rent a U-Haul truck to carry it all, and instructed them to list what items they wanted. I told them that I could get anything from TVs to stoves, refrigerators, and dishwashers, but that I had to have a deposit from everyone when the orders were placed.

That evening, people came to Greta's place with their orders and money. The dealers offered drugs as deposits, and I accepted. Around 7p.m., I lied and said that I was going to meet my partners and pick up the merchandise. I said that the truck would be at Greta's house at 10:00. I lied to my customers and headed home to pack. I had to get to the Greyhound Bus Station in time to catch the 9:50 bus to Chicago. I wasn't worried about Linko anymore. With all of the money that I had made that day, I had more than enough to pay him. I had plenty of drugs too. I was literally snorting heroin while walking down the middle of the street.

Marcus and Jeri's brother Jeff were home when I got there, so I went into the bathroom and snorted some more boy before coming out to pack. When Jeri came home she asked me what was going on. I told her that I was leaving. She tried to talk me out of it. I could tell that she was hurt. She had wanted so badly for us to be a family again, but I was not a family man. I was a dope fiend, a con man, a liar, and a thief.

I called a cab to take me to the bus station. While I waited, Jeri continued trying to talk me out of leaving. I was actually surprised. After everything that I had put her through, I thought she would be glad to see me go. I suppose, despite everything, she still loved me. I loved her too. Just not the way she wanted me to.

Jeri asked me to call Andi to let her know that I was leaving. I did. I said good-bye to Jeri and Marcus, then got into the cab and left.

At the bus station, I learned that I had just missed my bus. The next one wouldn't leave until 11:00, an hour after I was supposed to meet everyone at Greta's place with their stuff. That was the longest hour of my life. I was hoping that no one would catch on and come looking for me, but had it been my money, I would have checked the bus station before looking anywhere else.

I reached Chicago early the next morning, found Linko, and paid him the money that I owed. Ralph had moved off of Christiana and into Auntee's building. I moved in with him because he had two bedrooms. I got a job as a forklift driver at Handy Andy's, one of the local hardware chain stores. I collected unemployment checks, welfare checks, and food stamps as well. I stopped smoking crack when I left Detroit, but soon started speed balling again.

Tadpole was still working at the county jail. We would get high together in the evenings and on weekends. Sometimes we would go to his house to get high and play ping-pong. His wife, Doris, would cook for us, and we would have a good time. Doris would drink beer, but she didn't do any drugs. She and Tadpole had a good relationship, but Tadpole's drug use was really taking its toll on him.

One day Mother called with bad news. Aunt Jessie had passed away. I didn't make it to St. Louis for her funeral, but made sure that Ralph was able to go. Not even a month later, Mother called again. My cousin Tyrus had passed due to complications brought on by alcohol. In a single month, Nita had lost both her mother and oldest son. I didn't make it to Ty's funeral either, but again ensured that Ralph was able to make it.

One day, when I got to work, I learned that I was being "let go." They never told me why, but I suspect that they found out about my record. In any event, this was the first job in a long time that I hadn't been fired from because of theft. I decided to try truck-driving school. I enrolled in Train-Co, a black owned school on South Cicero. It was a three-month course, and although the school had been around for years, it went out of business after my first month there. I was on a roll.

181

THE HOODLUM PREACHER

A family living on the second floor of our building was evicted for not paying their rent. I moved into that apartment, so that Ralph's daughter, Nooky, and her boyfriend, Tommy, could move in with Ralph. I got another job working at the Radio Shack on Cermack, but after a few weeks, was fired from there too. I needed money, so I started hustling, selling drugs, and running con games on Auntee and anyone else who would listen to my lies.

I hooked up with another junkie named Chuck. We got high together quite a bit and became a good hustling team. When he lost his apartment, I let him sleep on my couch for a few days. One day, Chuck tried to talk me into burglarizing one of his friends' apartment. He said that he would boost me up to the window so that I could get in, told me what I could find, and where I could find it. I had two problems with that plan. Number one, I was not a burglar, and number two, the dude could have been home. I didn't do it.

A few weeks later, I told everyone that I was going to St. Louis for a few days. I changed my mind at the last minute, but didn't tell anyone. The day after I supposedly left, I was sitting in my living room eating a sandwich, when I heard someone kicking at my back door. I turned off the TV, grabbed a baseball bat, and stood behind the refrigerator. When the door finally opened and someone I had never seen before stepped inside, I started swinging. I beat him all the way down the stairs, nevertheless, he still got away. I saw Chuck standing outside around the corner. Although he denied it, I think he sent that boy to my house, thinking I was in St. Louis. I was through with him after that.

The first Sunday of November 1991 was a mild wintry day. I walked to 15th and Drake to cop a one and one. Between six and noon on Sunday mornings, heroin and cocaine were on sale. For every bag you bought, you got a second bag for half price. I made my purchase and began walking home. I passed a church on the corner and could hear that the morning sermon was from the fifteenth chapter in the Gospel of St. Luke. The preacher was telling the story of the prodigal son, "the lost son."

In it, Jesus said, *"There was a man that had two sons. The younger one said to his father, 'Father, give me my share of the estate.' So he divided his property between them.*

182

CHAPTER 8 - The Renegade

"Not long after that, the younger got together all he had, set off for a distant country, and there squandered his wealth in wild living. After he had spent everything, there was a severe famine in that whole country and he began to be in need. So he went and hired himself out to a citizen of that country who sent him to his fields to feed pigs. He longed to fill his stomach with the pods that the pigs were eating, but no one gave him anything.

"When he came to his senses, he said, 'How many of my father's hired men have food to spare, and here I am starving to death! I will set out and go back to my father and say to him: Father, I have sinned against heaven and against you. I am no longer worthy to be called your son; Make me like one of your hired men.' So he got up and went to his father.

"But while he was still a long way off, his father saw him and was filled with compassion for him; he ran to his son, and threw his arms around him and kissed him.

"The son said to him, 'Father, I have sinned against heaven and against you. I am no longer worthy to be called your son.

"But the father said to his servants, 'Quick, bring the best robe and put it on him. Put a ring on his finger and sandals on his feet. Bring the fatted calf and kill it. Let's have a feast and celebrate. For this son of mine was dead and is alive again, he was lost and is found.' So they began to celebrate."
(NIV)

Although it was raining and I had drugs on me, I slowed down to hear the sermon. I had heard the story dozens of times, had even preached it myself, but still, I found myself on those church steps crying in the rain like a baby. "Lord, forgive me. Please forgive me. I'm so sorry for the life that I've been living. Please forgive me."

I got rid of the drugs, went home and prayed even more. I realized then that I was that prodigal son. God had loved me and had done so much for me, but I had walked away from Him for a life that I believed to be exciting and fun. I realized that although I had walked away from God, He had never walked away from me. He had been watching over me all the time.

It was He who had protected me when I was in prison. It was He who had revived me every time I had overdosed on drugs. It was He who had kept people from killing me during the stick-ups at the drug houses. He loved me, and was constantly placing people in my life who would be instrumental in leading me back to Him.

When I first left the church, He sent Elder Campbell. When I went to prison, He sent Rev. Hodges. When I got out of prison, He sent Auntee, Rev. Rayford. When I was sitting on that bench in St. Louis after Dad had died, He sent Pastor Clark. Most often, He had sent my father, Rev. Burton Barr Sr.

I asked God to deliver me from the drugs and to change my life. Just like the prodigal son that Jesus had talked about, I was ready to go back home. I was finally ready to surrender everything to Jesus. I was finally able to fully understand the true meaning of the words in the song, "I Surrender All."

> "All to Jesus I surrender, All to Him I freely give;
> I will ever love and trust Him, in His presence daily live.
> All to Jesus I surrender, Humbly at His feet I bow;
> Worldly pleasures all forsaken, Take me Jesus, take me now.
> I surrender all, I surrender all.
> All to Thee, my blessed Savior,
> I Surrender All."

CHAPTER NINE

The Mission

The first thing I had to do was get out of Chicago. Almost everyone I knew there was in the game, in one form or another. Those who weren't, either didn't like me or didn't trust me; neither wanted me around. I had become that person parents warned their children to stay away from. So, it was decided that despite my legal situation, St. Louis was the best place for me. Mother, Nita, Christine, Sandi, and the others would form a strong support system. With my renewed dedication to the Lord, I felt that if I stayed away from the "Children Of The Night," I had a good chance of succeeding.

Sandi picked me up from the airport and took me to Mother's. I stayed with her for a few days, before moving into Christine's beautiful new house on the south side. Her teenage daughters, Tenesha and Tawana, had their own rooms, as did Terrell, her only son.

I began working in the shoe department of J.C. Penney's in Northwest Plaza. I didn't have a problem getting the job, since I had worked for them at another location in St. Louis. I knew that they would eventually find out about the Chicago incident and my arrest record. I also knew that the arrest warrants would soon catch up with me, but I wanted to make as much money as I could before they did.

I took a second job at the Toys "R" Us in the same mall. I didn't have a car, and the setup was very convenient. I had worked both jobs for a couple of weeks and was sure that things were going well, until one Friday, I left Penney's and walked over to my second job. When I got there, the manager informed me that my paycheck was in his office, and he asked that I go with him while he got it for me. I followed him to his office, but when I stepped inside, the door closed behind me. I turned around and saw the police standing there waiting. The manager handed me my check and I asked him, "Am I going to be able to walk out of here now?" I walked out all right - in handcuffs.

It seemed that I was wanted all over the eastern part of Missouri. There were warrants for me in St. Louis, St. Ann, Bridgeton, Maryland Heights, Richmond Heights, and several other municipalities, including some that I had never set foot in before. Apparently, while I was in Detroit, Chris and Irene had been passing bad checks in my name. For three days, I moved from one jail to another. After I was booked and processed in one jurisdiction, I would be held until officers from the next jurisdiction arrived to arrest me. Then I would leave with them. Finally, on that Sunday night, Christine and Mother picked me up from the Clayton, Missouri County Jail.

Shortly before Christmas, I was called into the personnel office at Penney's. I was told that they had received a memo about my having been fired from one of their stores in Chicago. I told them that I had never even been to Chicago, and that it must have been my brother using my name. Not long after New Year's Day, they got my record, and I got the boot.

During that time, Mother lost both of her brothers. The oldest, Uncle Archie, died just after Thanksgiving, and the youngest, Uncle Prince, died shortly after Christmas. Aunt Nini had gone blind, so Uncle Prince had been living with her. After he died, Christine asked me to move in with Aunt Nini to help her out. I moved into her basement.

I sold ads for one of the black gospel radio stations and got a job at one of the new Family Dollar stores. My work was so impressive that I was asked to manage one of their stores, but when they got the results from my background check, I was immediately fired and escorted from the premises because, as they said, I had falsified my employment application by not telling them about my criminal convictions.

I started getting discouraged, but Jesus knows just how much we can bear. It's kind of like Marine Corp boot camp. Sometimes we would be running up and down the hills and mountains, dressed in full combat gear with the hot, blazing sun torturously pouring down on us. The drill instructor knew just how much we could bear. When we got to the point where we couldn't go any further, and we were about to pass out or quit, he would hold up his hand and say, "Platoon, halt." When we are going through our trials and tribulations, Jesus knows how much we can bear. Sometimes we might get to the point where we feel like we just can't take any more, and we feel like giving up. That's when Jesus will hold up His hand and say, "Trouble, halt."

About a month later, I was hired at an upscale furniture store, Carafiol's. The company was owned by a Jewish family and had three stores in the St. Louis area. I didn't have to lie on my application because I never had to fill one out. As with many of the jobs that I'd had, I was the only black employee. I was also their top salesperson. During my first month there, I broke all but one of their sales records. I loved that job and the people I worked with. They eventually hired another brother, Stevie, and we became good friends.

I later went to court for the charges that were pending against me. I pleaded guilty and received three years probation with a seven year back up on what they call S.I.S., or Suspended Imposition of Sentence. If I successfully completed the probation, the conviction would not go on my record. Conversely, if I got into any trouble within the next three years, I would automatically go to prison for seven years.

I wasn't worried because I was determined to do what was right. Although I was no longer doing heroin or cocaine, I was still drinking and occasionally smoked marijuana. Truthfully, I didn't know that there was anything wrong with smoking weed, except for legality of course. As a matter of fact, sometimes when I got home from work, I would light up a joint and start reading my Bible while I was smoking it. I didn't know any better.

My success was partially due to my probation officer, Nancy McCarthy. I could tell that she really wanted me to make it, and I didn't want to let her down. My family also played a major part, but the biggest reason for my success was the relationship that I was forming with God. There was still a lot that I didn't know, and I messed up sometimes, but He was very patient with me.

I met a young lady at a nightclub and moved in with her, but after a few months, we realized it was a mistake. So I moved back in with Christine.

One day I started thinking about Bobby, and how God had saved his soul. He had drawn Bobby to Him before he died. I decided to call Pam, a friend of ours who lived across the street from Bobby and Irene and whom Bobby used to talk to about the

Lord. I had expected to hear her voice, instead Pam's mother answered the phone. She said that Pam was dead, but I misheard her. I thought she said that Pam was in bed. So I said, "When she wakes up, ask her to call me." She asked, "Who is this?" I said, "It's Bub." She said, "Bub, I said Pam is *dead*. She died a week after Bobby."

I felt so bad. I kept apologizing to her, but she insisted that she was all right. Pam had accepted Christ before she died, and I knew that it was because of Bobby. Pam wasn't my only friend that I later learned was dead. Butch had died from an overdose of heroin, Red was found in a hotel room with his throat cut, and Buck had suffered a stroke.

It was then that God delivered me from smoking cigarettes, and later marijuana. I was surprised because I had thought that I would be smoking weed for the rest of my life. I used to joke that I would be ninety years old and using my walker to go and get a bag of weed.

In 1993, Carafiol's announced that they were going out of business. They brought in a liquidation company to conduct the "Going Out Of Business Sale." The company was owned by a Jewish man named Mike, but was managed by a brother from North Carolina named Wes. Around this time, I went back to Morning Star Missionary Baptist Church, but left when I learned that Pastor Clark was no longer there.

Wes and I became good friends. He and his wife, J.J., had owned their own business in North Carolina. We talked about the possibility of me becoming one of their partners after the Carafiol's sale was over. I later got another job selling furniture at Dillard's Department Store in Northwest Plaza Mall. Jean, one of my co-workers at Carafiol's, had gone there and told the department manager about me.

In August, I received a call from Mother that completely messed me up. Fuzzy had died a horrible death. New dealers would sometimes come into a neighborhood and try to steal potential customers away from their regular dealers by giving away sample bags of heroin. One of them gave away some arsenic-laced sample bags on Christiana. One of those bags went to Fuzzy. His grandmother found him lying on the floor of his bedroom with the needle still in his arm.

On Saturday, January 1, 1994, God put it in my heart to be in church the next day. I didn't know where Rev. Clark was. So, I didn't know which church to go to. I called Nita, but she wasn't planning on going to church that day. I called her daughter, Patrice, but she wasn't going either. Nor was Christine.

I remembered Sandi having told me about a church that she had begun attending. I called her and she said the church was named West Side, and that it was at 4675 Page Blvd. She said that she would meet me there. But when I got there and saw how big that church was, I didn't want to go inside. I didn't like big churches, and figured that I would never find Sandi in a church that size, anyway.

Casting fear aside, I entered the building. I had decided that I wasn't going to like it, and when I walked in and saw all of those people, I immediately thought of them as a bunch of snobs. While the usher was leading me down the aisle, I looked into the pulpit and saw a young dude sitting up there. I didn't like him either. I said to myself, "I bet that's the pastor's spoiled son sitting up there, waiting for his father to die so he can take over the church."

The usher led me down to the third row from the front and directed me to a seat. To my surprise, I was seated directly beside Sandi. I sat down and we greeted each other. I asked her where the pastor was; she pointed to that young dude in the pulpit. That didn't make me feel any better, but as the services went on, I began to enjoy myself. At one point, all of the guests were asked to stand. When the people that I believed to be snobs began hugging me and shaking my hand, I said to myself, "These people are all right."

As the pastor preached, I saw something in him that I recognized. I had seen it in both Elder Kelly and Elder Campbell. I had seen it in Rev. Hodges and in Rev. Clark. I still didn't know what it was, but I knew that I wanted it too. Following worship, the pastor stood and greeted everyone. I introduced myself and told him how much I had enjoyed the service. He introduced himself as

Rev. Ronald L. Bobo Sr. and invited me to worship with them again. I assured him that I would be back.

I enjoyed myself so much that day that I went back that night for the 8:00 service. When I got to the church, I was surprised to find no one there. I called Sandi and learned that the 8:00 service was at 8:00am not pm I could hardly wait for Wednesday night Bible Study. I remembered the Wednesday night classes at Morning Star with Pastor Clark and hoped the class at West Side would be just as interesting. It was.

I loved going to West Side. Besides Sunday morning worship and Wednesday night Bible Study, there were also Sunday Morning Bible Study classes. A gifted teacher named Rev. Rosalind Denson led my class. Although everyone was friendly, it was two young ladies, Kim Rose and Gwen Wesley, who initially welcomed me to West Side and made me feel at home.

Things were going great for me. It had been more than two years since I had done any heroin or cocaine, and I had not been involved in any criminal activities. Nancy changed my probation status and transferred my files to an office on the south side. I was a member of one of the best churches in the country, and Wes asked me to go into business with him.

We rented an office in Ferguson and started "Carolina Credit Counselors," a credit repair business. Wes and J.J. were there full time, and I came in after working my shift at Dillard's. Business was lousy, so after a few months, we closed up shop and Wes and J.J. went back to North Carolina.

I became one of the associate ministers at West Side, teaching one of the Sunday morning Bible study classes. Wes and I kept in touch, and we constantly talked about business opportunities in North Carolina. Eventually, I decided to try it. I quit my job, packed up my things, said goodbye to everyone, and moved to Greensboro, North Carolina to go into business with Wes and J.J. Their home was beautiful. I moved into their basement and enjoyed the huge backyard and swimming pool. Things were really looking up.

My first Sunday in Greensboro gave me the surprise of my life. I was attending church with one of our clients. When she introduced me to her pastor, Rev. Johnson, I told him that I was from West Side Missionary Baptist Church in St. Louis. He shook my hand and asked, "How is Bobo?" I thought I had misheard him. I asked that he repeat himself. He asked again, "How is Bobo?" I said, "He's alright." At that moment, it became clear to me just how well-known Pastor Bobo was.

Greensboro was okay, but I missed West Side. I called Rev. Goatley, the well-read associate pastor from Kentucky, every week to see how everything was being handled. If I didn't talk to him, I talked to someone in the front office. After staying in North Carolina for a while, Wes and I rented a booth at a church convention in Manhattan. We went into business merchandising Dr. Martin Luther King Jr. statuettes. Unfortunately, that business flopped too. A few months later, I decided to go home.

The trip back to St. Louis wasn't an easy one. Wes' son had been using my car while we were in New York. When we returned to Greensboro, I found the front axle on the car damaged and one of the wheels leaning. I had nearly eight hundred miles to drive. They warned me against driving the car so far in such bad condition. I only had about $80.00, and gasoline was an issue, but I was determined to try it anyway. In hindsight, I made it back on a wing and a prayer.

I left Greensboro at about 4:00 that Monday morning. I was worried about the axle breaking but even more worried about gas. By the time I reached Fairview Heights, Illinois, the tank was empty, and I didn't have any more money. Although I was only 30 miles from home, I knew I wouldn't be able to make it unless I came up with a plan.

I had my old checkbook in the glove compartment, so I pulled into the Fairview Heights Mall, went into Venture's Department Store, and wrote a $10.00 check for something small. I returned the item at the customer service counter and received a cash refund. I bought $5.00 worth of gas and drove home. My sister Shirley had moved into Christine's spare room, so I stayed with Mother for a while. Nita had an extra bedroom in her apartment, and let me move in with her. We got to be really close. She was like another mother to me. I spent a lot of time with Nita's daughter Patrice (Patty) and Patty's two children, Quincy and Maya.

THE HOODLUM PREACHER

I went to West Side on Wednesday night for Bible Study and was greeted at the door by Rev. Denson. She told me that they didn't have anyone to preach the opening sermon. Pastor Bobo always asked that one of the associate ministers gain more experience by preaching a short message before Bible Study. She asked if I had a message to deliver. That night, I preached about how I made it back to St. Louis. Since I was no longer a criminal, I mailed Venture's a money order to cover the bad check that I had written.

One day, Pastor Bobo called me into his office and asked about my goals as far as the ministry. I told him that I wanted to start my own church, after learning as much as I could from him. I thought that was what preachers did. They sat under their pastors for a few years, and then left to become pastors themselves. Did I have a lot to learn.

During one bible study, I gave my testimony of how God had delivered me from a life of drug addiction and crime. I explained how I had been arrested more than 30 times and how God had still loved and watched over me, even when I didn't know it. I hadn't known how blessed I really was.

Shortly after that, Pastor Bobo called me into his office and asked that I take over leadership of West Side's Prison Ministry. Until then, it had been led by the church's Women's Missionary Union (WMU). The WMU went to the workhouse once each month and to the state prison in Jefferson City once every year, but Pastor Bobo wanted to take the ministry to a higher level.

I didn't know anything about leading a prison ministry. If I knew nothing else, I knew that having been in prison didn't qualify anyone to lead a prison ministry anymore than having been to grammar school qualified someone to teach the fifth grade. I knew that I wanted to do the best job that I could. Dad had always drilled into Ralph's and my head, "If a task is once begun, never leave it till its done. Be the labor large or small, do it well or not at all."

I started my ministry by working with Kerry Turner at the St. Louis City Jail. Kerry headed the prison ministry for Blessed Hope Missionary Baptist Church under the leadership of Pastor Herman Toles, one of my mentors. Deborah, the church's administrator, and Rev. Goatley heard about the Coalition Of Prison Evangelists (COPE). COPE, a worldwide Christian organization whose members had once been imprisoned, returned to the prisons to reach other inmates and tell them about the love and saving grace of Jesus Christ.

West Side sent me to the COPE convention being held in Orlando, Florida. I gathered all of the information that was available and talked to men and women who had practiced years of prison ministry. I listened to the guest speakers, Bishop T. D. Jakes and Jim Baker of the now defunct PLT Club. I had the opportunity to meet Chaplain Ray, publisher of many of the books I'd read while in prison, honest testimonies of ex-offenders who had become saved while in prison; and spent hours talking with and gathering valuable information from Jesse Mathes, founder of "Jesus Is The Way Prison Ministry" in Champaign, Illinois.

When I returned to St. Louis, I called Jesse. He invited me to visit his office in Champaign. I drove down and welcomed the chance to see his day-to-day operation. That evening, before I left Champaign, I told him my testimony about a preacher by the name of Rev. Hodges who had visited Chicago's Cook County Jail in 1985 and led me back to Christ. When I finished my story, he picked up the phone and dialed a number, then said, "Jerry, I've got a young man sitting here in my office who says you changed his life." He handed me the phone, and to my surprise, Rev. Hodges was on the line. It had been 10 years since we had spoken. We talked for a few minutes then exchanged phone numbers. It was truly a miracle. After 10 years, God had reunited me with my mentor.

I took my newfound knowledge back to St. Louis, and West Side's Prison Ministry exceeded all expectations. God gave us favor with Penney Hubbard, the volunteer coordinator at the workhouse. Instead of visiting monthly, we went every week. Claude Wills, a member of West Side, was employed at the St. Louis County Jail. With his help, we began conducting weekly Bible Study classes there. I asked Rev. Moses Townsend to be my assistant, and he arranged for us to visit the Jefferson City Correctional Center. With Pastor Bobo's permission, I named the prison ministry New Hope, and the number of volunteers increased to more than 30.

West Side's Prison Ministry was becoming known all over the St. Louis area. I knew it was not my efforts, alone, that made it possible. I was extremely grateful for the struggles of the women of the WMU. Mothers Gertrude Temple, Estelle Harmon, Ethel Waters, Jesse Dinkins, and Marie Goodwin had been going into the jails and prisons when I was still a runny-nosed junkie.

I still needed money, so Lee, my former supervisor at Carafiol's, got me hired on at Crossroads, which later became known as Rhodes Furniture Company. After a couple of months at Crossroads, Mike, liquidator of the Carafiol's going-out-of-business sale, told me about a position at another furniture store. I rented an apartment in one of Mike's buildings, and transferred to Quality Furniture because his son John owned the company.

My job at Quality Furniture was demanding, but my mission was crystal clear. God had told me that He was going to send me back into the jails and prisons to rescue His people, and He did. He sent us into prisons all over Missouri and Southern Illinois. I was being called on to preach and share my testimony at youth revivals and rallies. God was using us in ways that went beyond my wildest dreams. But the best was yet to come.

CHAPTER TEN

The Beginning

In May of 1999, God put it on my heart to leave my job and go into ministry full time. I went to Pastor and told him that I was leaving my job. He asked me how I was going to eat. I told him I wasn't worried about how I was going to eat when I was out there druggin', so I'm not going to worry about it now.

Truthfully, I was a little worried. As sales manager, I had been responsible for five stores. I would be leaping from a $24,000 salary and company car into a ministry with no salary at all. I didn't know how I was going to pay my $400.00 rent every month. I didn't have any savings. All I had was faith.

On July first, I put my trust in God and walked away from Quality Furniture. I gave up my apartment, moved into Christine's basement, and immediately went to work at West Side. Rev. Goatley let me share an office with one of the other employees. Within the next few days, God blessed me with several opportunities. Rev. Sammy Jones, president of our state convention, appointed me assistant director of the state's prison ministry. I worked under Millie Morris, a very dedicated worker out of Kansas City, Missouri.

A few months later, I was hired at West Side on a part time basis. I loved the ministry so much that I worked forty, sometimes even fifty hours per week on a part time salary. God rewarded my faith and faithfulness by blessing the ministry tremendously. It wouldn't be fair to take all of the credit. I was blessed to have some of the best volunteers working with me. I can truly say that they made me look good.

God continued blessing me. In 2000, I became an official employee of the West Side Missionary Baptist Church and member of the pastoral staff. I was appointed Executive Director of Great Things Incorporated Foundation, West Side's community development corporation. I was later appointed Director of the Missionary Baptist State Convention of Missouri. Under the direction of Rev. Anthony Kelley of Baton Rouge, Louisiana, I became one of the Commissioners of Prison Ministry for the National Baptist Convention. I was called upon to help establish prison ministries across the state of Missouri. New Hope was invited into institutions all over the country.

I had the honor of preaching at my cousin Nita's Going Home celebration; she died from cancer. I loved Nita very much and took her death hard, but Patty was devastated. Darron, Nita's youngest son, brought his new bride Nicole in from Florida. He and his brothers honored her by wearing tuxedos to the funeral. Not long after that, Aunt Nini died. I preached at her funeral too.

God took the prison ministry to a new level. He teamed us up with Brother Boogie, an old bank robber named Michael Anders. Brother Boogie had gone to prison after robbing banks to support his gambling habit. While he was incarcerated, God saved his soul. When he got out, he started an aftercare ministry to help others after they, too, were released. After having a hard time getting the support that he needed, he came to me for help. It became a partnership that was made in heaven.

Brother Boogie helped me to realize the importance of aftercare in the perspective of prison ministry. Churches can go into prisons and lead men and women to Christ, but without a support system upon release, their chances of going back are much greater. I should know, my experiences in 1986 are proof. Together, we teamed up with Nathaniel Johnson and Tony Gray, heads of prison and aftercare ministries, and Brad and Kathy Lambert of Connections to Success.

God continued to elevate me. I was elected Faculty President of the Berean District's Leadership School. I was appointed vice president of Congregations Allied for Community Improvement, CACI. I became chairman of the Law and Order Committee of the St. Louis Clergy Coalition, co-chair of the Eastern Missouri's Coalition to Abolish the Death Penalty, and director of the Berean District's prison ministry. I was even able to go into the Cook County Jail and minister with Rev. Jesse Jackson. That just goes to show you what God can do when you put your life into His hands.

God transformed me from a hopeless, dope shooting, street hustling, jailbird and con man, into a well-known and highly respected community leader. But I wasn't perfect. I knew that I had made many mistakes along the way. Although God had delivered me from many things, from time to time I still battled one demon. Alcohol.

My pride and reputation didn't allow me to seek the help that I needed. I didn't want anyone to know that I wasn't perfect. They couldn't know that I had a weakness. Instead of talking to someone, I preached sermons called "The Closet," "Super Saint," and "I've Fallen, and I Can't Get Up." No one knew that the preacher was talking about himself.

I don't know why God allowed me to struggle with alcohol for so long. Maybe He wanted me to know that I hadn't yet "arrived," and that I wasn't "The Great Rev. Burton Barr, Jr." that people had been telling me I was. Maybe it was because my compassion for alcoholics was insincere. I had more respect for thieves, murderers, and prostitutes than I did for alcoholics. There were times when I refused to be around my own brother because of his drinking. So, I couldn't let anyone know that I, too, was drinking. I was too ashamed.

My drinking had reached a point where I started making bad choices. I did stupid things that could have cost me my testimony, my ministry, and even my life. I thank God for His grace and mercy. I thank Him for friends like Pastor Bobo, Rev. Denson, Rev. Goatley, Ron, Terri Stearns, and my spiritual little sister, Rev. Dinah Tatman. These friends noticed that I was acting uncharacteristically, and wouldn't leave me until they had learned why. Then they loved me with the love of Jesus Christ.

Since I began writing this book, I have been blessed even further. In 2003, God brought Charlotte back into my life. We hadn't seen or spoken to each other since working together in Detroit back in 1968. Over the past 35 years, we had occasionally thought about each other, but made no attempts to find one another. She began to think about me more and more in August of 2003, and decided to see if she could locate me through the Internet. She did.

Amazingly, while I had been writing about her, she had been having strong thoughts of me. She called West Side and left a message on my voicemail, inquiring as to whether or not I was the person she had worked with in 1968. I called her back immediately, knowing that God had brought us back together for a reason. After daily conversations and occasional visits, I expressed my love to her and proposed on Thanksgiving Day. We began making plans for a 2004 Valentine's Day wedding.

Charlotte and I were married at Faith Tabernacle in Highland Park, Michigan, the same church where I had been assistant pastor when we were dating in 1968. Rev. Thomas had passed away many years earlier, and his son Ricky has since become the pastor. Pastor Bobo flew in from St. Louis and performed the ceremony. Many of my friends from St. Louis also made the trip, including Ron Cohen, who was my best man, and his wife, Katie.

My marriage with Charlotte has helped me to gain a whole new family, including five wonderful daughters, many grandchildren, and a great-grandchild. God also brought Andi and Marcus back into my life. When Charlotte and I reconnected in 2003, she encouraged me to locate my children. I learned that Andi was still living in Detroit. After fifteen years of little or no communication, we were reunited. I spent some quality time with her, when she and her three lovely daughters visited me at Charlotte's home in Highland Park on Christmas day of 2003. Shortly thereafter, I spoke with Marcus. God also restored my relationship with Everett. Even Jeri and I are on speaking terms again.

On Good Friday of 2004, I sat in church listening to Pastor Bobo preach one of the last words of Jesus Christ, when my cell phone started vibrating. When the service ended, I stepped outside to check my messages. Mother had passed away. Someone at the hospital had left the message on my voice mail. The only thing I remember after that is my spiritual big sister, Rev. Jean Hardge, hugging me and repeating that everything would be fine.

Pastor and Sister Bobo went to the hospital with Charlotte and me to view Mother's body. Although she hadn't been a member of West Side, we had her funeral at the church; Pastor Bobo delivered her eulogy. Mother had always been the one to inform me of someone's death. And now she was gone. My friend Vernon passed away too. I went to Chicago to preach at his funeral. Many friends that I had grown up with were in attendance and heard me preach for the first time.

This may be the story of the hoodlum preacher, but it is not simply my story. It is my testimony. God has truly been good to me. He has blessed me in more ways than I could have imagined. Some of the roads were rocky, but I've never had to walk them alone. God has been with me every step of the way. Like the songwriter said, "I've had some good days, and I've had some hills to climb. But God knows what's best for me, and He loved me even when I didn't love myself." So, I can say without a doubt: God is not only good, he is truly awesome.

Oh. I forgot to mention the most important thing. I found what it is that Pastor Bobo has. What it is that Pastor Clark, Rev. Hodges, Elder Campbell, and Elder Kelly possess. I found what it is that made them so different and set them apart from some of the other preachers that I have known. They are filled with the Holy Spirit. And I've got news for you. The Holy Spirit is not just available to pastors and preachers. He is available to you, too. *"How much more will your Father in heaven give the Holy Spirit to those who ask Him." (Luke 11:13b)*

Just remember, no matter what you have done, who or what you have become, God still loves you. *If we confess our sins, He is faithful and just to forgive us our sins, and cleanse us from all unrighteousness." (1 John 1:9)*

It doesn't matter where you are in life, whether you are in prison, on drugs, or living in a world of hopelessness. You don't have to let where you are, dictate who you are.

There was another thing that my father taught me. He said, "Son if you slip and fall down in the mud, don't just lay there and wallow in it. Get up, clean yourself off, and keep going. If you fall down again, get up again. If you keep falling down, keep getting up."

So my advice to you my friends is to put your trust in God. He is the only one who is able to keep you from falling. *(Jude 24)*

God loves you, and His grace is sufficient.

May the peace of the Lord be with you.

THE BEGINNING.

THE HOODLUM PREACHER

**Coming Soon From
BURTON BARR JR.**

YOU DON'T HAVE TO LIVE LIKE THAT: 7 Steps to
Changing Your Life

Book In Stores April, 2007

www.kobaltbooks.com